P9-CEG-779

Breaking UP

He's Just Not That Into God

Stina Wilson

Kregel *Publications*

Breaking Up: He's Just Not That Into God
© 2007 by Stina Wilson

Published by Kregel Publications, a division of Kregel, Inc., P.O. Box 2607, Grand Rapids, MI 49501.

All rights reserved. No part of this book may be reproduced, stored in a retrieval system, or transmitted in any form or by any means—electronic, mechanical, photocopy, recording, or otherwise—without written permisson of the publisher, except for brief quotations in printed reviews.

All Scripture quotations, unless otherwise indicated, are from the *Holy Bible, New International Version®*. Copyright © 1973, 1978, 1984 by International Bible Society. Used by permission of Zondervan. All rights reserved.

Scripture quotations marked KJV are from the King James Version.

Scripture quotations marked MSG are from *The Message*. Copyright © 1993, 1994, 1995, 1996, 2000, 2001, 2002. Used by permission of NavPress Publishing Group. All rights reserved.

Scripture quotations marked NASB from the NEW AMERICAN STANDARD BIBLE, updated edition. Copyright © 1960, 1962, 1963, 1968, 1971, 1972, 1973, 1975, 1977, 1995 by The Lockman Foundation. Used by permission. (www.Lockman .org)

Scripture quotations marked NLT are from the *Holy Bible*, New Living Translation, copyright © 1996, 2004. Used by permission of Tyndale House Publishers, Inc., Wheaton, Illinois 60189. All rights reserved.

Library of Congress Cataloging-in-Publication Data
Wilson, Stina.
Breaking up: he's just not that into God / by Stina Wilson.
    p. cm.
    Includes bibliographical references.
    1. Man-woman relationships—Religious aspects—
Christianity. 2. Mate selection—Religious aspects—
Christianity. 3. Christian women—Religious life. I. Title.
BT705.8.W55 2007
248.8'43-dc22   2007004892

ISBN 978-0-8254-3937-7

Printed in the United States of America

07 08 09 10 11 / 5 4 3 2 1

This book is dedicated to my younger brother Colton, who has given me some of the best relationship advice. I love you, and your strength and wisdom amaze me.

I would also like to thank my family for their love and support, and Erika for her unending editing help and God-given friendship.

OVERTON MEMORIAL LIBRARY
HERITAGE CHRISTIAN UNIVERSITY
P.O. Box HCU
Florence, Alabama 35630

Contents

Introduction

Every time I hear the words to the song "Come, Thou Fount of Every Blessing" by Robert Robinson, the knot in my throat burns as I try to hold back tears:

> Prone to wander, Lord, I feel it,
> Prone to leave the God I love;
> Here's my heart, O take and seal it.[1]

We are distracted easily. Many things tempt us to "wander from the God we love," and for women the temptation especially includes the male of the species. I almost let the worst tragedy become reality; I almost forgot God in order to be in love with a guy.

He wasn't a *bad* guy; he just wasn't a guy who loved God. Having a new faith, I barely knew how to follow after God myself, so how could I do it while dating someone who didn't want to . . . at least not now . . . maybe later? It was a wrenching decision to pull away from a guy I loved like crazy to go deeper with a God whose love I'd barely tasted. There were times when "letting go" of this guy felt more unbearable than the thought of giving up my relationship with God. I write this book because you, too, may have a nagging feeling that something isn't right between you, your boyfriend, and God. Maybe you've already broken it off, yet you feel like you're plodding through a desert yearning for a river. Maybe you're questioning your decision to break up. Or perhaps you're terrified that Grandma bought you this book because "God would want you to break up," and *you* beg to differ.

I was desperate for answers. I searched high and low for some "loophole" that would let me keep my boyfriend *and* God. I was bogged down in confusion, and I'd loosen my grip on my guy just to tighten it again. I was angry. I scoured the Christian bookstores, looking for something I could relate to my situation, but I found only books on dating. If I was going to find answers about dating someone who wasn't into God, I'd just have to investigate the topic for myself, using my Bible, my journal, and my Creator.

Despite the pain and chaos of letting my boyfriend go, I finally got the idea that falling in love is incomparable to a life with God. I took what I thought was a risk, and gave up someone in the physical realm to be with Someone invisible. I told God I wanted an adventure and received much more than that. I now know we're created for abundant life, yet unless we take the sometimes painful steps to receive it, we'll never feel the fireworks inside us that God longs to set off.

Dear "Jason,"

When I decided to love you, I loved you like we'd be together forever. It didn't cross my mind that we might end. I see now that first love is the most powerful kind because it is innocent and knows no boundaries. You were the first one to steal my heart, and for that I will never forget you. I now know why God advises us to be with one person for the rest of our lives; we deeply attach and it's not natural to rip loose.

I realize now that breakups cause more than pain. When we broke up it built walls and scars, and it created fear for future love. I don't know if you will read this book, but in case you do, it is important to me for you to know that you played a huge, influential role in my life. Documenting our past has revealed how much our relationship shaped who I am today. I write you this letter because I want the readers to know you are a wonderful person. We simply could not continue to pull each other in directions neither of us sought to go. Our paths overlapped for a time but eventually split apart.

A tree cannot grow beneath another tree's shadow, so I guess I had to find a place for my roots to grow and a position where I could soak up my own sun. You represent a friend who was there during the most fragile part of my life, and you let me go so I could grow. Thank you for putting up with me and for forgiving me for the hard times. You will always hold a place in the deep part of my heart.

Thank you for allowing me to discover who I am and to follow my greatest passion. I know you will do the same.

Love,
Stina

Discovering the Love of a Guy
chapter one

My head bounced as I gazed out of the bus window at the Philippine countryside. The palm trees, rolling hills, and little grass huts reminded me of a travel brochure. The monotonous sound of the bus engine was lulling me to sleep, and I was about to doze off when Seth, who was part of my mission team, sat down in the seat next to mine.

"So, Stina, if you could have any guy, what would he be like?" This was an uncomfortable question. Seth knew I'd come to a new understanding about God while training for this mission trip, and he'd heard that I was struggling with some boyfriend issues. Yet, coming from someone I didn't know very well, his question took me by surprise.

I knew, though, that Seth's question was one I needed to answer. I'd never really given it much thought. Before I became a Christian, I could date anyone I liked. Yet now that I had a relationship with God, I wanted Him to be my life's purpose. So anyone I dated should have his purpose in life rooted in God, too.

I thought about all the qualities I wanted in a guy. *Hmmm, good looking, smart, loving, hard working* . . . But my current boyfriend *had* all these qualities, yet something was still missing. I blurted out, "Well, it would be great if he loved God."

I waited for Seth to tell me why he'd asked such a personal question.

"But you don't believe you can have someone like that, or that kind of guy is possible to find, right?" He stated this as a fact, not a question.

"I guess I've never met anyone who has all the qualities I want and who also loves God."

Seth continued, "Have you read the verses that say that if God has given us His only Son, what good gifts will He not also give? He works all things for good for those who love Him, and He gives us the desires of our heart?" (see Rom. 8:28, 31–32).

"Well, I think—"

Seth interrupted, "Which one is it—you don't believe what God says is true, or you don't believe that He'll follow through?"

For someone who barely knew me or my situation at home, he had a lot of guts. I raised my voice in defense. "Well, yeah, I do believe what He says, but . . ."

"But what?"

"But . . ." He had me tongue-tied. I realized that no explanation would satisfy him.

Before I could say anything more Seth rose and looked at me. "You know," he said, "I'm not trying to judge you. I just want you to think."

As Seth walked away, I tried to justify my relationship with my boyfriend, Jason. *It hurts too much to think of not having Jason in my life. I love him. We have the same friends. Our relationship is comfortable. He's a good person, and we have so much history together.* I closed my eyes, trying to fall asleep, yet the thought of not having my boyfriend in my life haunted me. My mind drifted back to the day Jason and I met.

I hated PE class. I dreaded it with every bone in my body. It's cruel to force insecure grade-schoolers to sweat in the middle of the day and then make them go to the next class smelling like moldy gym shorts. I was twelve years old and in my second day of sixth grade. The bell rang and, hearing our cattle call, all the sixth graders shuffled into a locker room. I had no idea that my attitude toward gym class was about to change for an *entire* year.

As I turned the corner, my frown transformed into a grin that almost hurt. All of the yelling and giggling faded into silence; the crowd of gangly twelve-year-olds causing the havoc seemed to disappear. There he was, the man of my dreams. I felt like a pirate who'd found a treasure; I had never laid eyes on such a beautiful sight. Jason was everything I'd dreamed of.

His quiet self-assurance showed with each confident step. With his sagging pants and baseball cap turned sideways, he captured my complete attention. Even from across the gym, his big brown eyes sparkled like gems. I could tell he wasn't like all the other boys; I knew he was different. While love made others blind, it allowed *me* to finally see clearly, and my twelve-year-old eyes saw perfection.

With a dreamy smile I thought, *Maybe gym class won't be so terrible after all.* For the next few months I watched him from a distance. Little did I know it would take two years to finally get his attention.

During those years we occasionally hung out with the same friends. Secretly I was bursting with desire to be his girlfriend. But to him I was like a mole you suddenly discover on your arm. "Has it always been there or did it just pop up?" I didn't know that he knew I existed until a phone call during my eighth-grade year.

My mom's voice echoed up the stairs, "Stina . . . the phone is for you."

"Okay, hang on," I yelled back.

Sitting on the carpet in my room, I stretched for the phone. "Yellow!" I blurted into the receiver, thinking it was one of my friends.

To my delight, a boy's voice replied on the other end, "Uh, hello . . . is this Stina? Um . . . this is Jason, Jason Jansen." I bit my lip and jumped to my feet like I'd been stung by a bee. I managed to reply calmly, acting as if I wasn't *quite* sure if I could place him. "Oh . . . you mean the Jason in Mr. Burt's class? Oh, hey! How are you?"

By this time I was pacing the length of my room, back and forth from my bed to my closet. The sound of his voice was gracing *my* phone in *my* room. I couldn't believe it!

He continued, "Uh . . . yeah, I'm good. How are you?"

"Oh . . . I'm *pretty* good," I answered, trying to make my voice even.

"Hey," he suddenly asked, with no hesitation, "what are you doing on October 25?"

Not realizing what glorious event was on that day, I replied, "Uh . . . I dunno . . . isn't that a little far away?"

"Well, it's the Spirit Week dance, and I really want to go with you."

Squeezing the receiver until my knuckles turned white, I replied with a steady voice, "Yeah, I'll go with you."

I arrived at the dance with visions of busting it like a rock star until the sun came up. There was just one problem: I'd never slow danced with a guy. Suddenly I was gripped by fear. *What will it be like to be that close to someone? What if I do something stupid? Maybe we won't have to dance. Guys don't like to dance anyway.*

The hardwood floors vibrated as the disco ball sprinkled specks of light over our faces. The resounding echo of "Ice . . . Ice Baby" filled the room. I noticed a prominent separation in the room: to the right, girls whispered and giggled; while on the left, guys shuffled their feet, hands in pockets and shoulders slumped.

Before I had the chance to navigate around the room and prepare myself for the unknown, I heard a cough and turned. "Hey, d'ya wanna dance?" All the blood rushed to my face, my eyes widened, and all I could say was . . . "No."

"What do you mean, 'No'?" he asked, grinning with the right side of his mouth and one beautiful eyebrow raised. "I thought you said you wanted to come with me."

The blood in my head slowly drained back into the rest of my body. "I mean I'm thirsty," I replied. "I want to get a drink first. I'm going to go get a Coke."

Turning abruptly, I left him standing alone and hurried to the Coke machine. Taking as much time as possible, I fed the coins in, one—by—one. *Why am I so nervous? I've been waiting for this moment since sixth grade. Okay, go out there and just go for it.*

Embarking upon uncharted territory, I took a deep breath and headed back to the dance. Searching faces to the left and right, I couldn't find him. Then couples separated in front of me, opening a perfect path for me to see him . . . dancing with Stephanie!

Stephanie was *that girl.* Yeah, the one every jealous onlooker watches from the corner of her eye. The girl that's cute even when she burps. She could get away with not taking a shower in the morning and end up inventing a new hair trend . . . "the greased look." Yet the worst part of it was her kind heart. Even if I tried to hate her, I couldn't. She was undeniably sweet.

My heart dived to my stomach. I walked closer to make sure it was actually them. Yep, it was definitely Stephanie . . . and *my* date. At first I was hurt, and then I became angry. *If he wants to dance with her, let him. In fact, he can be with her all night. If I leave, he won't have the privilege of dancing with me. He's going to feel stupid when he realizes I'm not even here. He'll think I never came back from the Coke machine. It'll look like I was the one who rejected him.*

The click of my high-heeled sandals echoed down the empty hallway. I made my way toward the pay phone as fast as my legs would take me. Hastily, I shoved in quarters, then my voice cracked and tears trickled down the receiver as I asked, "Mom, will you please come pick me up?"

I waited all day Saturday, all day Sunday, and until fourth period on Monday afternoon for some sort of apology. I made sure to arrive fashionably late to class that day. Before entering Mr. Burt's classroom, I peeked through the window. There he was. *Oooohh, why does he have to be so cute!* I strutted to my desk making sure I looked everywhere except at Jason. Just as I was about to sit down he started to walk my way.

"Hey, where did you go on Friday?" he asked in a friendly tone, as if *he* was willing to give *me* the benefit of the doubt.

"Where did *you* go?" I snapped back, whipping my head around to give him a long glare.

"I—was on—the dance—floor—waiting—for you," he said, pausing between the words in irritation.

"Yeah, I know . . . with Stephanie!" I shouted as everyone in the class turned to look at us.

He tried to defend himself, but I interrupted each excuse. I made up my mind to have nothing to do with a guy who held an interest in someone else, and I refused to speak to him for the remainder of the year. I'd catch myself, though, from time to time, looking at him from across the football field, at a basketball game, or in a classroom. Yet it would be another two years before I'd dismantle my wall enough for Jason to peek over.

By my sophomore year of high school, I felt that I'd been on too many dates with too many guys, and in my ripe old age I was finally ready to settle down. The weekend was quickly approaching, and rumor had it that Jason was having a party at his house.

The night of the party, a few of us girls met up in Laura's room to get ready. Five different perfumes hung heavy in the air. Laura was wrapping her ponytail in a scarf. Danielle was looking in the mirror, pulling on her eyelid and carefully drawing lines from one corner to the other. I was smothering my arms and legs with fruity lotion. Danielle focused intently in the mirror as she tightened her lips to paint them with ultra shiny lip gloss.

"Hey, can I use that, Danni?"

"Sure," she said, as she threw the tube into my lap from across the room. "Who do you think is going to be there?"

Our minds raced as we thought of all the people we were about to party with.

"I know who *you* want to see," Laura said with a mischievous grin. Her dark, silky ponytail fell across her shoulder as she tilted her head to the side, waiting for my reaction.

Trying to hide a guilty smile, I said, "I don't know what you're talking about. I'm just going to have fun with you guys."

"Riiiiiiiiight," they sang in unison.

"Okay . . . whatever. Let's go!" I ordered.

My best friends and I looked stunning; we were feeling good as we pulled up to Jason's house.

Cars were lined up bumper-to-bumper in his driveway and spilled out onto the road. A cluster of familiar faces filled the doorway as well as a cloud of smoke that rose from their circle. They greeted us with pleased smiles.

We took a deep breath and opened the door, suddenly walking to the beat of slow, familiar music. I was so preoccupied with saying hello to everyone that I didn't notice Jason slouched in a recliner in the corner of the room. He and his friends surrounded the TV, watching Saturday Night Live, when I caught him looking at me. One of his friends tried to get his attention by hitting him on the shoulder and pointing at the TV. To me the room was suddenly silent. The low-lit room only enhanced the whites of his eyes as he kept staring. *He's not looking away . . . what does this mean?* Both of us hesitantly smiled and then slowly broke into full grins. Just when I was about to look away he patted his hand on his lap and motioned for me to come sit down. Like a deer deciding whether or not to cross a street, I finally made my move and casually walked over to his chair.

"Scoot over," I said with a smirk.

Butterflies took over my stomach as we sat, squished next to each other on his parent's recliner. The minutes melted into hours. We talked and laughed just inches from each other's face.

Without warning he looked down at my hand, slid his fingers in between mine and tightened his grip. Maneuvering my body to angle more comfortably toward him, I rested my head on his shoulder. Closing my eyes, I thought about the years of watching him, hating him, and wanting him. Breathing in the scent of his cologne, I couldn't believe where I was. Being so close to him made me feel as if I'd finally come home.

We stopped talking and people started to snore on the couch. Outside, engines started up and cars backed out of the driveway. I listened to his heartbeat next to my cheek. Maybe at that time I was too young to judge, but that night was the night that I'd always hoped for because that night I fell in love.

The right side of my forehead was cold from being pressed against the bus window for so long. My heart sank as I realized that I was now on the other side of the world and not in that recliner snuggled up with Jason. Suddenly my whole body felt cold. I wrapped my arms around myself, tilted my head against the seat, and wedged myself further into the corner. I hoped that if I sank far enough into my seat, I might escape my thoughts. I tried to forget what Seth had asked me. I couldn't decide which was worse: staying with Jason but never feeling fully understood in my new passion for Christ, or feeling the pain of letting Jason go, but feeling the freedom to walk down any path that God may lead.

> Jesus . . . said, "Then there's only one thing left to do: Sell everything you own and give it away to the poor. You will have riches in heaven. Then come, follow me."
>
> This was the last thing the official expected to hear. He was very rich and became terribly sad. He was holding on tight to a lot of things and not about to let them go. (Luke 18:22–23 MSG)

Sometimes people would suggest that I shouldn't be with my boyfriend anymore because he wasn't a Christian. But my initial reaction was, "You don't understand because you don't know how much I love him." I believed our love was greater than anyone else's experience of falling in love.

Falling in love is amazing, isn't it? People have been studying, singing about, writing books on, and making movies about love since God gave Adam a partner in the garden of Eden. Love causes us to act in ways that we don't recognize, do things we previously hated, and smile until our faces are sore. Letting go of such love is inexplicably painful, leaving a dent the size of a crater in the place where the love was.

My story, though, is only one among millions. Now consider yours. What are your reasons for holding on? Think about those hesitations and compare them to following Jesus, to knowing the *Creator* of love. We come to Jesus carrying all kinds of things; we hold tight to them. We see the unique power Jesus possesses, and our souls are uncontrollably drawn to Him. We come, asking if we can follow Him. We want to walk with Him, listen to Him, and learn what "real life" is all about. He looks into our eyes . . . and sees straight into the heart.

With our right hand we hold the person we love in a tight-fisted grip and with our left hand we reach out to Jesus and ask Him to fill us up. With desperation we say, "Lord, what do I need to do? I'm ready to follow You!" We get the same response Jesus gave to the official in Luke 18. God says, "Give up the things that keep you from Me and come follow Me." He longs to hold both of our hands so He can have *all* of us.

The following chapters hold my journey of letting go of a guy I dearly loved, to hold on to a God I longed to know more. Maybe you've already released a serious relationship, or maybe you're thinking about it. Wherever you are in your relationship, my prayer is that, unlike the official, you won't "walk away sadly" because the sacrifice is too great. My prayer is that you'll run boldly to Christ's side.

A Desire for More
chapter two

I don't know exactly how I ended up on that bus. But there I was, bouncing along the broken pavement of back roads in the Philippines. What I do know is the decision to trade a pantry full of gourmet food for a whole month and a half of PB&J sandwiches began with more than an itch to travel. It originated with an inherent longing for more. Not knowing what "more" looked like, yet compelled by a desire larger than myself, I packed my bags.

Do you ever feel that there has to be more to existence than "being in love"? Maybe everyday life seems monotonous to you. Being in a relationship may not bring the fulfillment you'd hoped it would. Are there areas of your life that you hoped a guy could fill but you still feel empty? God may be calling you to more than you're settling for, and you may be trying to ignore Him. Are you being called to rise up, move forward, live out your greatest purpose, and discover what true life is really about? To do that, it's crucial that you *first* discover a deep relationship with Christ *before* you get into a deep relationship with a guy . . . regardless of the cost. You may notice a tendency to ignore the "voice," yet you'll find that "whether you turn to the right or to the left, your ears will hear a voice behind you, saying, 'This is the way; walk in it'" (Isa. 30:21). You may find yourself at some point sitting quiet long enough to hear a voice that urges you to uncover your buried desire for more.

For me, the "voice" finally made it through a couple of months before I left for the Philippines. I'd dragged myself up the stairs of my parents' house at about three o'clock in the morning. My eyes were glazed over and my brain felt detached. Reaching the top of the stairs I caught a glance of my reflection in the bathroom mirror. I walked closer to it. Even though coming home late and stoned was now part of my weekly routine, what I saw in the mirror that night didn't look like me.

Black mascara smeared in the folds of my eyelids. Oil had collected in the creases of my face. My greasy hair was slicked back into what looked like a Koosh Ball on the top of my head. The cuffs of my jeans were caked in mud, my shoes were drenched from a rainy night, beer stains decorated the front of my shirt. My deep emptiness had finally surfaced, and I was forced to look at the disaster that was me. My vision blurred as I replayed a scene from earlier in the evening.

My arm is resting on the side of a ripped up greenish seventies couch. The aroma of marijuana and sweat permeates the air. Florescent lights filter through the smoke clouds that creep into the corners of the room. All around the room, people seem lifeless, like pieces on a chessboard waiting for a move, yet unable to go anywhere except endlessly forward and backward. A clump of bodies in front of me sink into cushions. Their eyes are closed, their heads rest on each others' shoulders. In the kitchen a couple of guys guzzle from a beer bong, throw their heads back and laugh in what seems to be slow motion.

One girl wearing a plastered smile clings with both hands to the corner of the wall as she watches a fly buzz around the room. With effort, I pull my gaze back into my lap. A blanket of loneliness covers me . . . where's

Jason? He said he might come. He . . . he must have stayed at one of his friend's houses. Tired of waiting, I lean forward to rise, and I leave. I leave in my white Adidas tennis shoes, smeared with mud from the bonfire earlier that night.

Dropping my toothbrush, I realized I was daydreaming. My watch read 3:45 AM. Trying not to wake my parents, I tiptoed into my bedroom and noticed the letters "H-O-L-Y" peering out from under a pile of books. I reached down and picked up the Bible my Grandma had given to me for Christmas. Flipping through the untouched pages, a sentence caught my eye: "You will seek Me and find Me when you search for Me with all your heart" (Jer. 29:13 NASB). *Hmmm, I wonder what that means.*

Although I had little practice at praying, something inside of me cried out for anything real. Getting on my knees and touching my forehead to the carpet I whispered, "God, if you're real, do something with my life. Please get me out of here . . . goodnight."

The next morning I sat in a chair outside on the porch, crunching down a bowl of Honey Nut Cheerios. As I gazed at the lake beyond the dock, I heard the sliding glass door open behind me.

"Stina," Mom demanded, standing with her arms crossed, "when did you get home last night?" She was wearing "mom pajamas" adorned with steaming coffee cups and the words "good morning."

"When are you going to get new pajamas, Mom?" I replied as I shoved an extra-large spoonful of Cheerios into my mouth.

Raising her voice and stepping in front of me, she placed her hands on her hips and looked me straight in the eye. "That's *not* what I asked you, Stina!"

"I dunno when I got home; I guess it was kinda late." I sat, staring at a lone Cheerio floating around in my bowl.

With a sigh she started in with the regular speech. "Stina, I'm worried about you. You can't be staying out late and sleeping in late. I woke up in the middle of the night again, thinking about you, and you *know* what that means."

I glanced at her to judge the severity of her anger; she hadn't blinked once. Her head was tilted to the side, and she was waiting for a response. She persisted, "Maybe you need a change in your life."

When my mom woke up in the middle of the night, thinking about one of her kids, it was serious. It always led to long letters of concern that awaited us on the end of our beds the following morning. I can't remember a time when she's been wrong about her suspicions. Receiving one of "the letters" was enough to make us kids feel as though we'd had an encounter with the Oracle on the *Matrix*. My mom has divine knowledge which only mothers are permitted to access; her letters have the amazing ability to stop any one of us in our tracks.

Suddenly, I set my bowl down next to me and looked her straight in the eyes. "I know, Mom, you're right. I do need a change. I want to go away from here . . . somewhere . . . anywhere, Mom!"

She sat on the armrest next to me and leaned in to put her arm around my shoulders. Squeezing me, she said, "Well, we'll figure something out. After graduation we can look around for something or . . . or maybe we could just go on a vacation."

Satisfied with my willingness to acknowledge her concerns, she stood up and walked back inside. Unsatisfied, I followed her in and made my way back up to my bedroom. On the floor next to my bed, I found the letter folded up. As I read the words from my mom, a girl I once had a conversation with came to mind. This girl had told me about her church and how they sent her on a trip to another country. *That's a good deal; maybe I'll check that out.*

A few weeks later I called my grandparents. They were members of the local church and had connections there. After I shared my idea with them, they were thrilled. I'd barely hung up the phone, and my grandparents were at my side putting a mission trip pamphlet into my hand.

"Three thousand, six hundred, and fifty DOLLARS?" I blurted. "I just got my paycheck, and you know how much it is? Seventy-six dollars, including tips!" I didn't realize I was shouting.

My mind spun, *I can't afford this! And how will I ever get accepted to go on a mission trip when I'm not even technically a Christian in the first place? Can I just tell them I'm a Christian because, after all, if my grandparents are, I am too?*

As I looked through the pamphlet, my grandparents hovered over me like I was opening a winning lottery ticket.

"Oh, honey," my grandma said, gesturing with her hands. "Usually kids your age write a nice letter to their friends and family; it's called 'raising support.'"

Suddenly fear came over me as I realized that this trip might actually happen. I thought about leaving my friends, family, and most of all . . . Jason. I hadn't yet considered the dramatic tragedy of being away from him. *NO . . . no way, I can't leave him. That would be way too long. I'd go crazy.* I began to reconsider the whole idea as I realized the sacrifice and the change I was about to make.

Looking at the floor, I tried to be sensitive. I was about to demolish Grandma's high hopes. In the sweetest voice possible I said, "I'm sorry, but I don't think it's a good idea." I gently placed the pamphlet back in her hand and got up to leave the room.

She looked as if that lottery ticket wasn't a winner, and she'd already started to spend the money. Not willing to back down so easily, she scrambled for a compromise. "Stina, just write the letters and if you get the money, you go. If not, you can forget the whole thing. Does that sound reasonable?"

The trip is only three weeks away. I'll never get the money in time. Let's see . . . one week to get the letters out, one week for a response, and one week to pack. NOT GOING TO HAPPEN. To relieve her disappointment I replied, "Okay, sure, why not."

"You've got mail" took on a whole new meaning throughout the next week. I'd never received so many letters at once in all my life. Those words, followed up by a sealed envelope in the mail, should have brought excitement, but instead they became the source of my anxiety. Every day after school I gritted my teeth at the echo of, "Stina, you've got mail!"

One hundred dollars . . .

Fifty dollars . . .

Three hundred dollars . . .

Two hundred and fifty dollars . . . on and on it went.

Opening yet another letter I prayed, "God, pleeeeeeez . . . I can't handle this. I really don't think I should go!"

Even before the dreaded "packing week," I received the last check, which put the total at two hundred dollars *over* the amount I needed in order to leave.

A week and two days before I was supposed to board the plane, I held a pile of uncashed checks in my hand. I had to make a decision whether to go or stay. *I can't let down all these people who are donating money, but I so badly want to run and hide.* I felt compelled, almost against my will, to make a change in my life, but underneath all of my fears was a curiosity I couldn't deny.

This turmoil felt like an uphill struggle, and reminded me of my car. It was a Jeep Wrangler with a four-cylinder engine and a lot of miles on it. My drive home from school took me up a long hill. It wasn't very steep, yet on some days it seemed endless. Each time I drove up this hill, I'd have to keep downshifting, and people behind me would honk their horns; it was frustrating and embarrassing. One day I said to myself, "Will I ever be able to get up this hill faster!?" And an answer came to me, "You will if you get a new engine."

In a similar way, a time comes when we must rip out our old way of thinking and receive new vision in order to move forward. Someone has said, "If we continue to do what we've always done, then we will continue to get what we've always gotten." The Bible tells us, "Don't copy the behavior and customs of this world, but let God transform you into a new person by changing the way you think. Then you will know what God wants you to do, and you will know how good and pleasing and perfect his will really is" (Rom. 12:2 NLT).

Ripping out the old and replacing it with the new might require some time in the repair shop, but in the long run we'll be able to travel more efficiently with greater speed. God yearns to exchange the way we operate for the way He operates. He says, "For I know the plans I have for you. . . . They are plans for good and not for disaster, to give you a future and a hope" (Jer. 29:11 NLT).

When presented with the opportunity to get away on a mission trip I was petrified, because I didn't know God well enough to realize that I could completely trust Him. The Lord reassures us, "As the clay is in the potter's hand, so are you in my hand" (Jer. 18:6 NLT). I was comfortable with my predictable life and didn't wish to give up my routine. And because I had limited vision, the Lord's perfect timing seemed out of sync with my life.

Change is almost never a comfortable thing, and even though it wasn't comfortable to pack my bags, I knew I had to go discover more—though I had no clue what that meant for my life. We may want to stay in the refuge in our safe harbor. Yet something in our souls cries out for change. We long to take the uncharted way, even though it may be rough and unsteady. Sometimes it's necessary to take a chance, to venture to the edge of our known world and find out if it's really flat. We suspect that if we take that journey, we may find something—we may find more, find freedom, find truth.

The most crucial part of the journey at hand is to raise the sails, make the first move forward into the unknown. If we never take a risk and instead continue to believe that the world is limited to what we know, we'll live partially, not fully.

Wherever we may find ourselves along life's path at this time, we have a God who is asking us for more. He is inviting us to trust Him a step further. He searches to find people who are willing to give up things in their lives to follow Him (see Mark 10:21).

God is who He says He is, and that means that you can fully trust Him with your life. As you embark on this new journey into discovering perfect, unconditional love for the first time, I ask you to step out and trust, to serve Him more . . . whatever that may entail. God created you to have a deep, unbelievably intoxicating relationship with Him. Let Him show you what real life is. Let Him whisk you away as He slowly reveals what lies beyond your current understanding.

Discovering God's Love
chapter three

Before my trip to the Philippines I had the wrong idea about unconditional love. I thought it meant loving someone despite how *bad* or *good* that person is. I thought of God like Santa, but more accepting—God would bring me presents without asking if I'd been good that year. I could crawl onto His lap and confess all of my horrible sins while still counting on Him to pull a present from His bag and hand it over with a jolly smile.

I came to realize that *unconditional* love means there are tons of *conditions*—besides my behavior—on which His love *doesn't* depend.

I discovered a new truth during training for the mission trip. Night after night I stood in a church, watching people raise their palms upward while they sang songs to a Jesus I barely knew. All I could think about was my boyfriend back home. Sneaking off campus regularly to use the pay phone was the only way to ease the ache of missing him.

I couldn't believe what I'd gotten myself into. I thought I'd signed up for an expenses-paid trip to see the *world*, not to see *God*. Instead, I found myself stuck with a bunch of "Jesus freaks" who always wanted to do everything together—even pray together. Sure, it was fine to pray before bed, but not every moment of every day. I'd always thought that God spoke in heaven, but not to me in daily life.

Every day we went out into ninety-degree weather to practice a skit, and if we weren't *doing* something for God, we were *talking* about God. If we weren't *talking* about God then we were *singing* about God. I felt as if I'd died and gone to God Boot Camp, and I was ready to forget the whole stupid thing.

One day on my "escape" to the pay phone (my only solace in this time of torment), my leader's hand clamped onto my shoulder.

"Where are you going?" she snapped.

"Um . . . to call my boyfriend," I replied, feeling like a dog with my tail between my legs.

"Follow me," she ordered.

Feeling like a prisoner who'd been caught scaling the prison wall, I trudged behind her. Leading me up the stairs, she suddenly stopped in front of a table. I stared at it, and she stared at me. Her eyes burned a hole right through me. The longer she stared, the faster my heart raced and the redder my cheeks became. A million thoughts raced though my head—*Why is she staring at me? Did I miss the rule in the mission trip handbook that read, "Thou shall not communicate with anyone besides the Lord thy God?" Maybe she's one of those prophets to whom God tells my innermost thoughts.*

"Stand up there," she said, interrupting my thoughts.

"Where? On the table?"

"Yes, get up there."

Confused, I obeyed, and climbed atop the table. I stood there, looking down at her.

"Okay, now try to pull me up," she insisted.

I grabbed her arms and pulled as hard as I could, but it was impossible to pull her weight from the ground.

"Keep pulling . . . harder!" she cried.

With all my might I tried to pull her up onto the table until I ran completely out of strength.

"I can't," I replied.

She raised her arms toward me again and said, "Okay, now let me pull you."

With her one tiny tug, I was back on the ground next to her.

"Do you get it?" she asked.

"No, I don't get it," I snapped. I didn't appreciate a stranger butting into *my* life. I was annoyed that she was playing some stupid game with me when I could have been talking to Jason.

"Don't you see?" she continued. "When it comes to faith, it's so much easier for someone to pull you down than it is for you to pull someone else up."

Okay. I saw what she was getting at. I'd made a tentative decision about Christ, but my relationship with Jason was based on who I was before that. When I was with Jason it was easy to forget my faith and revert to my old way of thinking and acting. It wasn't that Jason was a bad person; it's just that I was a sort of fledgling Christian and I needed to know my weaknesses.

It was as if my leader had pressed a button that read, "Don't push or an explosion will occur." I knew she was right but I wasn't ready to hear it. I thought about how much I loved Jason, and I was scared of how my life would change if I truly gave this God thing a chance. Suddenly overwhelmed, I collapsed onto the floor in tears. Somehow I knew that this trip would be a time of emotionally letting go of a guy I loved so that I could fully be taken into God's arms. I was about to discover a different kind of love . . . God's unconditional love.

Later that night it was time for worship again, and this time my attitude had softened. *Okay, God, if You're real, if You're really all that these people say You are, show me.*

Walking toward the door of the church, a thought came into my mind: *Don't look at people; look at your Creator.* That gentle thought set the stage for the night that would change me forever. I like to sum it up using the phrase my dad often uses: "It was the first day of the rest of my life." Better yet, a *new* life began that evening. When the music started, so did an internal struggle. After a forty-five-minute wrestling match with God, He pinned me. I found myself in the position of surrender under His bittersweet words . . . "I promise."

But, God, what will I do without him? "I promise." *What about all my friends?* "I promise." *But God, I'm not strong enough.* "I promise." *But, but . . .* Again, "I promise." These were the words I heard after every desperate question I brought to the Lord that night.

Not only did I sense God speaking to me, but for the first time in my eighteen years of living I finally understood why people raised their hands to God as they sang. I could finally understand my grandma's desperate attempts to make sure I got "saved." For the first time, I felt an indescribable love poured out on me. I experienced the reality of the Creator's powerful capacity to invade a simple life like mine.

With my stringy hair plastered to my cheeks, I knelt on the floor. Tears cascaded down my nose, ran off my knees, and gathered onto the carpet beneath me. It was as if I'd forgotten where I was, who I was, and all that surrounded me. One thing I knew for sure, however: the God of the universe loved *me*.

It was amazing; the sudden realization of God's love instantly erased thousands of condemning thoughts and words I'd piled onto myself. I thought about His endless pursuit, the time He invested into getting me to submit to His love and listen to the words "I love you. I love you. I love you. I love you." At that moment I realized that my shame mattered only to me, not to my loving Creator.

The only thing that concerns Him is that we arrive at the place where we can hear and believe that He loves us *unconditionally.* I'd believed in my mind that God loves me, but I'd never really let it penetrate my heart. God, though, will move mountains to get His love to travel from our heads to our hearts. Despite any condition we find ourselves in, God will go to extreme measures to get us on our knees, listening, and accepting His love for us.

A band called Third Day sings,

> I've heard it said that a man would climb a
>   mountain
> just to be with the one he loves. . . .
> I've never climbed the highest mountain
> but I walked the hill of Calvary.
> Just to be with you, I'd do anything.
> There's no price I would not pay. . . .
> I would give my life away. . . .
> I know that you don't understand the fullness of
>   My love
> how I died upon the cross for your sins. . . .
> But I promise, I would do it all again.[1]

It is Christ's love that initially draws us to Him and when we receive even a glimpse of its power, we cannot help but be melted. As we enter into a personal relationship with Jesus Christ, everything in this world slips into perspective. Our priorities change, and suddenly we sing with passion that same song back to Him . . . *just to be with You I'd do anything.*

While I was kneeling and weeping on that carpet, I remember thinking that my life finally made sense. I remember knowing for a fact that God predestined me to be kneeling on the floor of a small church at that moment. I felt fully that I was born to know the love of my Creator. Today the simple truth still blows me away—the God of the universe loves me unconditionally. If you, too, deeply believe this, it's impossible to escape the transformation that instantly occurs.

If you're thinking of breaking up, though, because you heard it's the "right thing" to do, and not because your love for God draws you to do His will, then please *stop.* Evaluate your relationship with Christ as well as your motive for doing the "right thing." His love must be the foundation of your relationship with

Him as well as with others. Empty works are a gas tank running low, yet works fueled by Christ's love endure until the end.

> For Christ's love *compels* us, because we are convinced that one died for all, and therefore all died. And he died for all, that those who live should no longer live for themselves but for him who died for them and was raised again. (2 Cor. 5:14–15, italics added)

To understand His love for us, we must begin at the good ole rugged cross. Most people have heard of Christ's death more than once, whether at Sunday school or from Mel Gibson's *The Passion of the Christ*. The cross where Christ died represents the very core of the Christian faith. You probably understand that Christ died for everyone's sins, but what you may not get is that Christ died for *you*.

That fact didn't touch the core of my soul until I allowed myself to be affected by it. Before, the cross had always felt so impersonal. When people would say, "Jesus died for all the sins of the world," I'd think, *Well that's great. But how do I know that He wasn't thinking more about Martin Luther King Jr. than about me when He was dying there?*

On my quest to understand the cross, and after much prayer and conversation with others, something became clear to me; the cross is both universal and personal. It's for everyone, but it's also for me.

Let me explain the universal by using a rock concert as an example. I've always hated concerts but never understood why. I thought I must be a boring person until I realized that I didn't like them because they were impersonal. The universal is like being part of the crowd at the concert. People are everywhere, and they are people who need stuff. They need to go to the bathroom, they need food and water, and there are long lines so they must fight their way to the front. Then they have to find places to put all their leftovers. They end up throwing it into a big pile that really stinks. They consume, only to make a mess, and then do it all over again. And I become just one of them.

Hearing that Jesus died for all the sins of the world made me feel I was just another needy person for whom Jesus had to die—just another face in the crowd at the concert. The lead guitar player may have seen me from the stage but likely didn't notice. What I really wanted was a backstage pass. I wanted to come face-to-face with *the man* and be someone important to him. I wanted to shake his hand and look into his eyes long enough so I *knew* he saw me. I wanted him to offer a personal invitation to an after party. If I was going to be just another anonymous crowd surfer, I'd rather stay home.

To meet Jesus face-to-face, He has to be revealed to each of us, individually and personally. That's what Jesus was getting at—and what Peter got—when Jesus asked His disciples, "Who do people say the Son of Man is?"

> They replied, "Some say John the Baptist; others say Elijah; and still others, Jeremiah or one of the prophets."
>
> "But what about you?" he asked. "Who do you say I am?"
>
> Simon Peter answered, "You are the Christ, the Son of the living God."
>
> Jesus replied, "Blessed are you, Simon son of Jonah, for this was not revealed to you by man, but by my Father in heaven." (Matt. 16:14–17)

Watching Jesus mangled on a cross on the big screen may not have brought us to our knees. Why? Because only God—not a Sunday school teacher or Mel Gibson—reveals to us who Jesus is. Apart from the work of God in our hearts, no human, book, film, or story can bring us to our knees before the King. God gives us that backstage pass to the concert to meet "the man"; and after coming face-to-face with Him, every word He sings becomes deeply personal.

With longing, God has looked down on His people and desired to be close to us. But He couldn't take us into Himself because He is spotless and we aren't—because of our sin. There was only one way to do it. He loves us so much that He came down as a perfectly clean sacrifice to offer what we need; He took on all of our junk, removing the guilt from our dirty hands, making us righteous, and allowing us to hold hands with God for eternity.

> God made him who had no sin to be sin for us, so that in him we might become the righteousness of God. (2 Cor. 5:21)

True, Jesus died to save the world and forgive all sin, but there's also something very personal to this saving: He wants to enter into an intimate relationship with you and me. Before reading this next section please quiet yourself, pray that all distractions leave your mind, and ask the Lord a few questions:

1. What is it in *my* life that You died on a cross for?
2. When You were on the cross, were You thinking of me? What were You thinking?
3. Will You help me to understand the cross in a personal way?
4. What do You like about me?
5. Why do You love me personally?

Write down whatever comes to mind, even if you feel like a lunatic . . . just please write it down.

Christ's death not only removes sin, it puts us in a relationship with Him in which He alone can fill gaps that we are incapable of filling. Here are some examples of the kinds of gaps that only Christ can fill:

- Father Gap: His death allows you to have a fatherly relationship with Him, despite an absent or dysfunctional earthly father.

- Image Gap: His death replaces every ugly word against you with a thousand "you're beautifuls" from the One who created beauty.
- Worth Gap: His death proves to you that there is no price high enough to measure your worth.
- Wound Gap: He died for you so a hurt that won't seem to heal can finally be mended by the One who makes us whole.
- Hope Gap: He died for you so you could finally understand the reason you were born and believe you have hope and a future.
- True Love Gap: His death puts an end to the pattern of trying to earn love through good behavior and good deeds, allowing you to rest in His unconditional love.

After a few tries, I finally broke up with Jason, and I remember feeling completely alone. I felt like I was just another face in the crowd, that I could never be individually and personally loved again. But at the time I didn't have an accurate view of God's love for me. It's vital to know God's love personally; it allows us to easily weigh the difference between God's love and a guy's love.

One really big difference is that God's love is eternal.

> And I am convinced that nothing can ever separate us from his love. Death can't, and life can't. The angels can't, and the demons can't. Our fears for today, our worries about tomorrow, and even the powers of hell can't keep God's love away. Whether we are high above the sky or in the deepest ocean, nothing in all creation will ever be able to separate us from the love of God that is revealed in Christ Jesus our Lord. (Rom. 8:38–39 NLT)

Unfailing love is one of the ways in which God loves us. Babies, at about five months old go through a stage called separation anxiety; a baby believes that if his or her mother leaves the room, she ceases to exist. It's amazing that even from the time we're born, we have an innate need for love, and that never stops. Babies have no inhibitions, and they're not afraid to cry long and loud when they think they've been left alone. But as we grow up we tend to hide our deepest longings. The Lord loved us as He formed us in the womb, and He will continue to love us after the grave. We can rest in the knowledge that His love is eternal and no passing human love can compete with it.

Another difference between a guy's love and God's love is that God is the source of all love.

> God is love, and all who live in love live in God, and God lives in them. And as we live in God, our love grows more perfect. (1 John 4:16–17 NLT)

While people may have ulterior motives that fuel their actions, God loves us purely just because He *is* love. He has no motive other than it's His nature to love. He alone is the bottomless "love source" into which we dip our tiny cups. In other words, we cannot expect a *creation* (a boyfriend) to give greater love than the *Creator* (God) can give. His love is very different than ours. His love is blind to many of the reasons why we love people, like outer appearance, intelligence, money, smooth talk, "how he makes me feel," talents, and much more. When we dip into the true source of love, "our love grows more perfect." If we learn how to love from the Creator, we're capable of loving people more fully, and we'll also know the love of others who know God's love.

So a final way that God's love is different from a guy's love is God's love is unconditional.

> This is real love. It is not that we loved God, but that he loved us and sent his Son as a sacrifice to take away our sins. (1 John 4:10 NLT)

In the years since "God Boot Camp," I've thought I was in love a few times. I don't have enough fingers for the number of times I thought I'd found real love, and then discovered that the guy didn't meet my needs the way I wanted, or that he wasn't "my type." Many definitions try to capture the meaning of real love, but in spite of a thousand recipes on how to make true love, people are still hungry for the real thing. Some people try to fill the empty feeling with junk food—one-night stands, serial relationships. Our misunderstanding of true love is developing a world of people literally starving to be loved unconditionally.

If you ever feel like an anonymous face in the crowd, the truth is that God has never taken His eyes off you. God is intimate; He longs to perform a concert of love songs to you only. This is love—that before we even knew we were loved He died for us, in spite of our inability to adequately love Him in return. We are simply unconditionally accepted, adored, and paid for with a price that no boyfriend could ever afford.

Why Should I Break Up?

chapter four

In trying to find a solid answer to *why* I should break up with my boyfriend, I asked a lot of people this question: "Now that I want to fully love God, why can't I love Jason, too?" Most people responded with, "Because the Bible says so." Once in a while I'd hear, "Because you're unequally yoked," and I'd think, "What do eggs have to do with anything?" What I didn't get was an explanation of *where* or *why* the Bible says so or what exactly "unequally yoked" means. I was being asked to give up something important—my relationship with my boyfriend, and I felt like I deserved more than "because I said so" or an egg thrown in my face.

So I did some research of my own, and here's what I found out. "Unequally yoked" is a phrase that comes from a verse in the King James Version of the Bible: "Be ye not unequally yoked together with unbelievers." In the more modern language of the New International Version it says, "Do not be yoked together with unbelievers" (2 Cor. 6:14).

Imagine two oxen joined together at the neck by a wooden crosspiece so they can pull a plow. They are two animals of the same species, joined together to accomplish a certain job. They've been trained to respond to the farmer's voice, and they're considered a team once they are joined together by the yoke. A wise farmer will pick two animals that work well together, that have about equal strength, and make a good team.

If one animal is stronger, more stubborn, or lazier than the other, one of them could get hurt, and they're likely to end up walking in circles. A "team" like that is more like a pair in bondage. Paul uses this illustration to instruct us to be careful about who we "yoke" ourselves to in any kind of relationship that will shape our identity or the way we do things. The application to romantic relationships is obvious since they're the relationships that impact us the most.

If we try to live life yoked together with an unbeliever, it's nearly impossible to enjoy harmony and agreement. As a team of two, both must be unified in their destination. When the two oxen are pulling in different directions, they're fighting against each other and the struggle weakens both of them. To stay tied together is foolish. Their ultimate goal will not be accomplished.

When God comes into our lives we start to see life through His eyes. Our purposes, passions, and priorities change. Even if we don't yet know exactly what those priorities are, life itself has greater value simply because God is in it. We have greater confidence in what we can accomplish, because we know that it isn't done by our strength, but by God's. We know that anything is possible if God is in it.

As a result, you may suddenly find that things you used to care about—goals, perhaps, that you and your boyfriend had together—now don't matter. You start reevaluating what you love, and you're drawn to care about what God cares about. You're motivated by your love for God, and your desire to please Him comes from your love for Him. Things that neither you nor your boyfriend ever cared much about now mean everything to you. God may call you to move, start a ministry, feed a homeless person, and your boyfriend now sees you as crazy because you obey Him. But in reality, your eyes have opened to life in terms of eternity.

We discover things about life, too, through knowing Christ, things that God "reveals" to us through His Spirit. Suddenly we start saying things like "I've been created for a purpose and I'm accountable for living it out" or "I need to forgive, and I don't have a choice about it" or "All people are measured by God; why should I care what any person thinks about me?"

We want to talk about these things, share these thoughts with others, or even shout about them. But how are you going to feel when you express these things to the most important person in your life, and he stares at you with a blank look on his face? The tension created by this disconnect is likely to make you talk less about God—and worse, to notice Him less in your life.

If you sense this is happening in your relationship, it's not just a feeling. It's a warning. Perhaps it's time to unhitch yourself from the yoke before you do great harm to yourself and the person you love.

At first, I couldn't pinpoint what was so frustrating about trying to persuade Jason to see things my way. I wanted him to understand this new path I'd found and agree to walk down it with me. But like the oxen, we were pulling in different directions, and with every attempt at persuading him to change direction, I was weakened, and I miserably failed.

I now see the difficult situation I put myself in. I was not only pulling against my boyfriend, I was struggling to hold up my relationship with *God*, a relationship with my *boyfriend*, and *my boyfriend's relationship with God*. The burden became too great, and sooner or later, one of them had to go.

I had a real awakening one Sunday after my mission trip. After church, I went home and sat on my porch. The birds were chirping, and it was a beautiful afternoon. I asked God why it was so hard to convince Jason that knowing Him was a wonderful thing. I started to journal, and I sensed God's response to me:

Listen to the birds . . . Can you understand them?

No.

If you wanted to tell them about Me, could you?

No.

I send birds to minister to the birds. If you tried to tell them about Me and My love, what would happen?

I'd get frustrated and give up.

Yes, because I haven't given them the understanding and the knowledge of your language. I'd have to open their ears, prepare their hearts. I must be at the foundation of all you do and say, or you might as well be trying to communicate with birds. It's noise not comprehended; it's nonsense to their ears. I must be at the foundation of all your life and ministry. The house will collapse without a strong foundation.

I realized that I was frustrated because Jason and I were speaking different languages. As much as I tried to get him to agree with me, nothing I said worked. I realized it didn't matter how much I preached and prodded—unless the Holy Spirit was the one who persuaded Jason, nothing would be accomplished. It was by the Holy Spirit prodding *me* that *I* came to know God, so how could I expect it to be any different with Jason?

If you and the person you're dating do not have a foundation rooted in loving Christ first, the relationship you build won't be stable. This instability will soon turn into a deep dissatisfaction. Any material discontent you've ever struggled with does not compare to the vacancy you'll feel when God's purpose in your life is being wasted.

Jesus says that His yoke is easy and His burden is light. The only way that the burden can be light is if you give this burden to the Lord. The weight of trying to hold up both your own and your boyfriend's relationship with God is too heavy, and soon enough, one relationship will come crashing down.

At one time I thought that Jason and I had so much in common, and that the way we looked at faith was the only thing we didn't have in common. So why couldn't we keep our relationship and work around this one difference?

But what did we have in common that *really* mattered? When it comes down to it, someone who's serious about following Jesus doesn't have that much in common with someone who isn't. "Oh," but you say, "there are so many things we have in common: we like the same food, sports, entertainment, and intellectual activities."

Of course, this can be true. You can be in harmony with almost all of life's goals. But life goals are much different than life purpose. Goals are something you do; purpose is who you are. If knowing God is the main purpose of your life, it's devastating when you can't share this with the person closest to you.

Yes, you can fall in love with an unbeliever. But when it comes down to what really matters, the two of you are speaking different languages. You two are like the oxen going in circles: you think you're getting somewhere but you keep ending up in the place you started. You love your boyfriend, but you also love God, and the pull of them both will get you nowhere.

After the initial excitement of being in love wears off, you'll find yourself longing for intimacy that you can find only with someone whose life is firmly rooted in a foundation in Christ. When your life is rooted in Christ you have a whole different purpose for living, and suddenly you find yourself feeling alone in that purpose.

Because your views and desires have changed, neither of you feels free to share the deepest longings of your heart, and neither of you feels understood by the other. There's no solid common bond to keep the two of you together. Your fulfillment now lies in your relationship with God. This presents a problem because your boyfriend's satisfaction lies in you. You're looking to God for fulfillment and your boyfriend is looking to you for fulfillment. Trying to make your lives fit together is like trying to put a square block into a round hole. God created us in such a way that only when we look to Him will we truly be satisfied.

Here's another answer I found to why I should break up with Jason:

> The oak tree and the cypress grow not in each other's shadow.[1]

If you've never heard the term "missionary dating," it means to date someone with the intent or hope of converting him or her. Sometimes our pride deceives us into thinking that we can date an unbeliever if we wear a messiah mask. We believe we can change someone, but it's God who does the changing. Missionary dating presents a problem because once we give our hearts and emotions away, it's extremely difficult to take them back even when we know we should. Pretty soon, we're desperately rationalizing the relationship.

Right after Jason and I broke up, I still felt enough emotional ties to spark a fire. I felt as if I were in one of those cartoons where the character has a demon on one shoulder and an angel on the other. Again and again I'd sit in the kitchen, staring at the phone from across the room.

"Call him," one side whispered.

"No, don't! Are you stupid?!" the other side shouted.

Being a person of weak will, I'd pick up the phone and dial the *oh so* familiar numbers. My heart would pound as I anticipated the sound of his *oh so* familiar voice. I'd try to justify my reason for calling. *It's okay. I'm inviting him to church!*

Oops, I was taking on the role of the Holy Spirit . . . once again! *Note to self:* If you find yourself rationalizing your relationship, chances are it's not a relationship you should be in.

After knowing I needed to drop it, I'd take the situation into my own hands anyway. I thought that if I didn't keep pushing God onto Jason, it might be my fault if he never came to know God. Before I picked up the phone, though, I should have asked God what He thought about it. But because I was afraid that God would tell me "No," I should have known that I was seeking my own will, not His.

So once again, I made the call.

"Hello." My cheeks felt hot, my ears burned, and my heart pounded so loudly I wondered if he could hear it through the phone.

"Hi," he answered in a monotone. "What do you want?"

Surprised at his irritation at hearing my voice, I replied, "I . . . uh, I . . . how are you?"

"I'm fine," he snapped.

The coldness in his voice caused my heart drop . . . for the millionth time. For some reason, I couldn't learn that calling him was a bad idea. It hurt to hold on to my feelings for him, but letting go hurt worse.

He continued, "I just don't know why you keep calling me when you're the one that broke up with me. It's like you're trying to torture me!"

"I'm sorry. I really am. I'm just having a hard time, I guess . . . I know that you said you weren't into the church thing the last time I invited you, but I thought . . . maybe you would change your mind?"

"No, no, no! I don't know how many times I have to tell you, Stina. You said it yourself; we're different now."

He was angry, and I didn't blame him. First I tell him that we can't be together, and then that I can't live without him. The Bible advises, "Let your 'Yes' be yes, and your 'No,' no" (James 5:12). Furthermore, our contact after we broke up was always on *my* terms. I made him feel like if he wasn't at church with me, he wasn't worth being in contact with. Not only was I hurting myself, but I was sending him the message that he wasn't good enough for me or God unless he met certain requirements.

I'd picked up the idea somewhere that God needed me. In reality, God needed me to back off. Sometimes the more we preach, the more we push away. I wasn't listening to the whisper that kept saying, "Let go, and let God."

The tears started, I sniffled into the phone, and soon I began to wail. I didn't understand why breaking up had to be so difficult.

Most people made it look like ripping off of a Band-Aid, but to me it felt more like open-heart surgery.

"I dust don doe dut du due!" I said breathing heavily, sniffling, and blowing my nose.

"Oh, don't cry pleeeeez. I can't handle this anymore! Okay, okay . . . I'll go to church with you. If that's all you want from me, I'll do it! It's not going to change anything, but I'll do it to make you happy."

My wailing slowly turned into a whimper, and I took him up on his offer. Like a scrounging seagull, I'd been circling this prey for so long that I didn't care what I caught . . . as long as it was something.

The smell of fresh paint and expensive cologne wafted past us as we sat down in the pew. I looked around the church with a glimmer of hope in my eyes. But Jason and I looked like one of those couples at the mall. The wife is ready to shop and excited to try on clothes for her husband. The husband is along for the ride but would rather be watching a football game at home. The wife doesn't know that when she's in the dressing room, he's sitting in one of the waiting chairs, and as the sales lady walks by she looks at him with a grin of compassion. This gives him the liberty to express what he's really feeling: "Yeah, I'll probably have six more hours of this!"

Every word the pastor said penetrated my soul. The worship music was like a refreshing rain. People raising their hands to God was comforting because I knew they were excited about God just like me. Every time I stepped foot in church it felt like coming home to Mom's home cooking—the familiar smells, being surrounded by people I trust, everyone hungry for our favorite meal. I just hoped Jason would feel this way too, and every time he didn't, I was very disappointed.

"So, what did you think?" I asked after the service, hoping to hear him say that he'd love to go again, and maybe we could go home and discuss the three P's in praying that the pastor talked about in his sermon.

"It was fine," he said in a solemn voice with straight face.

This seemed to be the tone of most of our "spiritual" conversations: *solemn* and *fine*. Never were they *great* or *exciting*. Never did they carry the tone of who God was to me.

> If our Message is obscure to anyone, it's not because we're holding back in any way. No, it's because these other people are looking or going the wrong way and refuse to give it *serious* attention. (2 Cor. 4:3 MSG, italics added)

No one can force someone else to want to know God personally. It's easy to make the mistake of thinking the reason your boyfriend doesn't understand your faith is because you haven't explained it clearly enough. Rather, maybe it's not that he doesn't want God in his life, but he isn't willing to give God *serious* attention. He's looking the other way. He knows that giving God attention means changing his life. Remember, God doesn't need us; we need Him. If people don't seek Him, they won't see Him: "But if from there you seek the LORD your God, you will find him if you look for him with all your heart and with all your soul" (Deut. 4:29).

Another reason to break up with someone who's not into God is the fall—not the big Fall of Adam and Eve—your fall. If you're trying to hang on to your relationship, maybe you're measuring your spiritual growth and accountability against your boyfriend's progress. If so, you're looking into the wrong mirror. There's the tendency to think that you are a "good Christian" simply because compared to your boyfriend, you *are* a Christian. There's a very real danger that, without even noticing, you could slide down a very slippery slope. You may fall so far from where you want to be as a Christian, you don't know how to start climbing back up again.

In science, the second law of thermodynamics states that, as time passes, anything left on its own will deteriorate and eventually break down. This also applies to relationships. After a while you may be tempted to compromise your faith in order to maintain a peaceful relationship. When you start to compromise, your relationship with God becomes weak and unnourished. Soon, you're not the only one frustrated; neither you nor your boyfriend feels free to be who you want to be without feeling judged.

You're still longing for someone to share your faith with, and he wants his old girlfriend back. Because you're both being held back from the things you want to do, bitterness and resentment enter into your relationship.

If each of you believes your way is better, you'll find yourselves on opposing teams. Soon, competition is the fuel for your relationship. He may feel that he's competing against God, your church, and your church friends for your love and attention; as a believer, your values and ideals will constantly be challenged as you spend time together. He'll always be trying to prove that he's just as happy as you are without being "religious." You'll want to prove that you have greater peace and purpose through God. All the competing to out prove each other will eventually cause bitterness between the two of you.

A final reason for breaking up with the guy who just isn't into God has to do with your future. "We'll stay together and he'll change later" is a mentality that will forever provide false hope for women. Many Christian girls are satisfied that their boyfriends don't seem to object to their Christianity. You might think that because he's tolerant and will even go to church, that is enough reason to stay together. He's a good person, and your only complaint is that he might stay out at a party occasionally. You figure that his having a few beers isn't enough reason to break it off. What you may not see is that the problem isn't his drinking beer; it's that his heart hasn't been transformed by the love of God.

But you figure that in the future you'll really get him "saved." The sad reality is, it's not as easy as you might think. As time goes by, his tolerance for your religion will eventually wear thin, even if you're married, and the tension between the two of you will surface.

Then, in times of trials you won't have the support you need from him. The difference in the way Christians and unbelievers respond to difficult times became real obvious recently. My little brother was diagnosed with cancer. One unbelieving friend said, "Tell your brother my strong thoughts are with him." My Christians friends said, "I'm praying for him." Thoughts are nice, but they won't heal my brother. My Christian friends know that nothing in their power will cause healing—only God can bring about healing.

If your boyfriend just isn't into God, when trials come, your sources of strength come from opposite places. He'll rely on himself, you'll rely on God. You won't be able to cry out to God together, and your faith might actually be undermined, not encouraged.

If you're not strong enough to break it off, you're probably not strong enough to win him for the Lord. I recently spoke to a girl who was once in this situation. She told me of her regrets and explained how being tolerant of her boyfriend led her to become a hypocrite. She thought she was strong enough to withstand the "pulls," but eventually she found herself barely hanging on to her own faith. She shared that her relationship was a sexual one. I could hear the shame in her voice as she explained, "After we finally did break up, I asked my ex why he never wanted to know God. He told me that if *I* had taken my faith more seriously, maybe he would have too."

In Jeremiah 29:11 God says, "For I know the plans I have for you . . . plans to prosper you and not to harm you, plans to give you hope and a future." You can't predict a good future based on a bad present. Who you choose to yoke yourself to is one of the most crucial decisions you will ever make. No one will step in and make the choice for you. If Christ is number one in your life, it's impossible to consistently keep Him there while dating someone who's disinterested in knowing Him. If you make excuses and procrastinate, you'll only prolong the pain.

Think about what you need to nurture your relationship with God right now. Try to set your emotions aside for a moment, and focus on what's happening in your relationship in the present. Will you continue to be tolerant of your guy's disinterest in faith but constantly pull against him because he wants to go in a different direction? Or will you be wise enough to unhitch yourself and gain the freedom to walk down the path God has for you?

Claim the fullness Christ is offering in His freedom. You'll survive the difficulty of the present, and you won't regret it in the future.

Breaking Up
chapter five

I was more than happy to be home from the Philippines mission trip. Adjusting my backpack, which was almost as tall as me, I scanned the baggage-claim area for a familiar face. My heart almost bounced from my chest when I saw him. Better looking than ever, holding a stuffed platypus and a bouquet of daisies, Jason walked proudly toward me. My mom and my best friend came into sight behind him. Running awkwardly because of the weight strapped on my back, I flung my arms around his neck. My instincts took over, and for an instant I forgot the sacrifice I was about to make as soon as we were alone.

"I missed you so much," he whispered in my ear.

Burying my head in his shoulder, I wondered if this might be our last embrace. His voice lulled me into the reality of again being in his arms. Suddenly I was flooded by questions from everyone at once.

"How was it?" Mom asked with a relieved smile, bending to pick up one of my bags.

"What was it like?" my best friend inquired. She studied my face, trying to detect how I felt.

"Are you tired?" Jason asked, as he put his arm around me with sweet concern.

Still smiling, I suggested we talk while we walked. We piled into the car, excited about catching up on all our news during the drive home. Being with the three most important people in my life made me feel incredibly blessed. Having my best friend as well as my mom in the car with me calmed my nerves.

At least they *will always be in my life*, I thought.

Gazing out the car window, I had never felt so comforted by the Space Needle's blinking light. I'd never appreciated the organization of our freeway system more than at that moment. Never before had my soul rejoiced at the thought of a Starbucks' mocha and a bug free bed. Chatter filled the air as I attempted to replay in detail the last three months of my life. As I recounted stories from my mission trip in the Philippines, in the back of my head I was haunted by the conversation to come with Jason.

Later that evening, we arrived at my parent's house. Jason and I finally made our way out to the porch where I couldn't seem to form a single word. My only comfort at that moment was the chirping of frogs and the rhythmic lapping of water against the dock. Jason sat in a chair next to me, and between us was a small, square table. Even though he sat a foot and a half away, it felt as if we were on different planets.

At that moment I longed for my life before knowing God. I thought back to all the time Jason and I had spent together: the hours just sitting and talking, the road trip to his grandparents' house, arguing whether we should eat at McDonald's or Red Robin, enjoying enchilada dinners at his parents' house. I thought about all that he'd done for me. He was there for me during my family problems, high school drama, and all the ups and downs of our relationship. My heart felt cold at the thought of never again being wrapped in his arms. Who would I call when I was annoyed with my friends and family? My heart burned as I thought of missing that faraway grin he gave me right before saying, "You are so beautiful."

What about the little things? I glanced over at him. He curls his toes under when he sits down. His strong hands seem always to protect mine. He spends more time on his hair than I do on mine. His deep brown eyes stand out even in a room full of people. His quirky mannerisms and witty comments make me laugh every time . . . he had no idea that the littlest things about him made me melt.

My expression couldn't hide the turmoil brewing inside. I could hear the blood pumping in my head. I kept my eyes focused forward and avoided looking at him. I drew in the familiar smell of his cologne as he reached his hand over onto my armrest. *How could I break up with someone I loved so much?*

"What's . . . what's wrong?" he asked, leaning in toward me. Attempting to ease the tension, he forced a smile but his eyes were filled with worry and concern.

Half of me wanted to leap onto his lap and never leave, yet the other half couldn't deny this "greater love" I'd discovered.

Glancing his way every so often, I finally began with a broken voice, "Jason . . . something happened while I was gone . . ."

"Yeah, so, I'm sure a lot happened, and I want to hear all about it. What's going on?" By this time he had both of his hands on my chair, reaching for my arm to hold onto.

Reflecting on the undeniable reality of God I finally burst out, "I know this sounds crazy! But for the first time in my life I realize that God is real, and He really cares about our lives, Jason. It's so powerful and I can't deny it. I mean, I believed in God before, but now I feel like I *know* Him. As much as I might try to deny His existence, I can't. It would be like saying 'water isn't wet.' That's how real God is to me now!"

Somewhere in the back of my head I hoped that my little speech would open the gates of heaven and pour down the reality of God on Jason.

Sensing that this might change our relationship, he looked at me with eyebrows etched in confusion. "That's fine and great, but what are you trying to say? What does that have to do with us?"

Looking at the ground, I quietly answered, "I . . . I don't know. I mean, I just don't think it's going to work between us. God has become the most important part of my life, and I know you don't see things the way I do in that respect."

Not fully taking me seriously, he said with a sigh, "Stina, I believe in God too, but it doesn't mean that we have to get all crazy about it. I'll support you in your faith, but I'm not going to go to church with you and all that. Old people go to church, and when I'm old I'll probably go to church too."

That mentality made me furious and I burst out in frustration, "Sure, why *don't* we do everything when we're old? Yeah that's it, we can start living our lives when we're about to die. It's just like you wanting to travel when you retire; we'll be *so* old that we'll sit on the beach all day with a margarita, 'cause we can't walk anymore. Jason, I want to live for God now! He's real *now*, and I wish so badly that you could understand that!"

At this point he realized how passionate I was about what I was saying. Desperately willing to compromise, he fished for some kind of happy medium.

"Okay . . . okay, so what do you want? I think we can work this out."

"Well, first of all, we can't have sex anymore."

Not missing a beat, he said, "Fine. I don't care. I'll love you anyway."

Surprised by his eagerness to comply (and suddenly confused), I continued. "You know what though? Loving God isn't about not having sex; it's about so much more. Let me be honest. I feel like I've learned a new language, one that opened up an entire world for me. The horribly painful part is, the person I'm closest to doesn't speak this language . . . so we can't communicate very well. I could try for our sake to speak my old language, but this new one just makes so much more sense."

He pulled his arms back onto his lap and sat straight in his chair as he stared ahead in silence.

I watched as he stood up, trying to hide the tears that brimmed in his eyes and threatened to spill down his cheeks. With his back to me, he walked down the porch steps. "Well . . . I guess I should go now. You can call me when you figure out if you can bring yourself to speak in your 'old' language."

This was going to be harder than I'd even imagined. Now *my* mind raced, trying to come up with a negotiation. *He's a good person. He's not an atheist. Maybe I'm being selfish. God has grace, so maybe I should too. Maybe if I get him to go to church with me he'd change his mind once he sees that church isn't what he thinks it is. He might actually like the music. If I pray hard enough, maybe the sermon will speak to him. Maybe I should give it a chance because if he's "the one" and I let him go, I'll regret it for the rest of my life.*

Exhausted, I slowly made my way back inside the house and into my dearly missed bed. *I'll figure this out tomorrow.*

In my opinion it's okay to procrastinate on cleaning your room because it doesn't necessarily hurt anyone. But postponing a breakup until a "better time" was one of the worst mistakes I've ever made. I not only prolonged my own pain but I basically lied to Jason by causing him to believe I'd consider changing my mind.

One definition of insanity is to continue to do what you've always done but to expect a different outcome. After a great deal of turmoil, I eventually became determined to take a risk and see where the road less traveled would lead me.

I want to help you navigate you way to the right path, so here are some lessons I've learned that can help your through the chaos of breaking up. My prayer is that you, too, will find yourself walking hand in hand with the Father, free of limitations and ready for the great journey ahead.

Then you will call, and the LORD will answer;
you will cry for help, and he will say: Here am I.

(Isa. 58:9)

I was so busy thinking about what *I* was going to say to Jason that I forgot to ask God what *He* wanted me to say. The first thing I should have done was pray. I wish I'd called on the Lord before initiating the breakup with Jason. It's important to pray before going into any life-changing situation. Jesus, who was the Son of God, often needed to get away and pray by Himself. It's easy to forget to talk to God when your mind is preoccupied. By meeting with God beforehand, you're inviting Him to be the center of the situation. Before going to the cross, Jesus fell to the ground and prayed, "My Father! If it is possible, let this cup of suffering be taken away from me. Yet I want your will, not mine" (Matt. 26:39 NLT). Before you break up with your guy, find a place where you can be alone with God. Be honest about how you're feeling and ask Him to give you wisdom along with the right words to say. As you *pray,* ask the Lord to be with you and to give you strength.

I can do everything through him who gives me strength. (Phil. 4:13)

I found it extremely difficult to look Jason in the eyes and actually say the words, "It's over." I was used to expressing only feelings of love or adoration. When I came face-to-face with him at the airport, I felt an agonizing temptation to ignore what I knew I needed to do. It just felt so good to wrap my arms around him again.

Do not think that you have to break up in person. Who made that rule anyway? Let's get real here: the focus of a breakup is not to be as polite as possible. I'm not saying another method makes the pain any less excruciating, but if a letter, a phone call, or an e-mail is the only way you can get through the break without falling apart, I recommend ending it *by any means possible.*

Two people can accomplish more than twice as much as one; they get a better return for their

labor. If one person falls, the other can reach out
and help. (Eccl. 4:9–10 NLT)

I was lucky to have a few amazing friends that respected and
understood my decision to break up with Jason. Even though at
times I felt like I was annoying them—constantly needing their
advice—they stood faithfully by my side. They offered insight,
Scripture, prayer, and listening ears. A great coping mechanism
might be hours of tearful conversations with your best friend.
Make sure you have at least one trusted friend who will pray and
process with you post-breakup. Be aware that some of your friends
or family may not understand or support the split. Make sure you
find someone who encourages you in your decision; ideally a pastor, mentor, elder, or close friend can be your *breakup backup*.

I am the true vine, and my Father is the gardener.
He cuts off every branch in me that bears no fruit,
while every branch that does bear fruit he prunes so
that it will be even more fruitful. (John 15:1–2)

I should have never let Jason walk off the porch that night without being clear that we were over and done. At the time, I chose to
let the breakup drag on rather than watch Jason walk away for the
last time. In lengthening the process, I prolonged the suffering—
for both of us—and sent myself spiraling into confusion. I began
to second-guess the breakup and lost sight of why I was ending it
in the first place.

The longer a wound is left to fester, the longer it takes to heal.
And while hurting myself, I hurt Jason, too, making him feel like
he was a piece of meat dangling on a hook, all in the name of
Jesus.

Expect the temptation to put things off until later. Even if
your emotions scream, "You can't do it!" recognize this as a lie
and focus on what you know you need to do, not what you feel
you want to do. "Be strong and courageous! Do not be afraid or

discouraged. For the LORD your God is with you wherever you go" (Josh. 1:9 NLT).

Some people choose to go the "just friends" route, but I strongly advise against it; being "just friends" is not making a clean cut. When a couple is in love and chooses to break up, it often takes a lot of time and healing before they can handle being around each other again. Emotions are raw, and the natural temptation is to fall back into the familiarity of acting like a couple again. Don't resort to calling your breakup a "break" from each other because you're fearful about losing him. The Bible does not say, "Let your 'No' be 'Maybe,'"; it says, "Simply let your 'Yes' be 'Yes,' and your 'No,' 'No'" (Matt. 5:37). If you have the hope of an eventual reunion in the back of your mind, that hope will prohibit you from truly letting go. By stringing him along even with loving intentions, you're hurting not only yourself, you're hurting him too. Avoid all of this and *make a clean cut*.

Surely you desire truth in the inner parts;
  you teach me wisdom in the inmost place.
(Ps. 51:6)

One of the biggest mistakes I made in the breakup process was preaching to Jason too much. I felt a knot in my stomach each time I spoke to Jason about God, hoping and praying that he'd "get it this time." My intention was never to be preachy; I just wanted him to know the indescribably beautiful God I had discovered. What I didn't realize was that my pressure on him to accept Christ was pushing him to reject faith. More often than not, you're setting yourself up for failure and disappointment if you try to preach your boyfriend to following God. You'll only "preach him away."

By pushing your faith on him, you may be unintentionally trying to play the role of God in his life. Remember that God is big enough to speak to him personally when the time is right. Even though you may feel that it's your responsibility to convince, know that it's the Holy Spirit who changes lives, not you. Explain your dedication to your faith in the best way you know how. Don't expect him to understand your relationship with Christ and your reason for breaking it off, and don't try to make him understand. The only way to prove that your faith is real is to live it out every day. Focus on nurturing your relationship with God and let go of nurturing your boyfriend's relationship with God. It's wonderfully normal to be excited about God, yet when it comes to conveying that excitement to others, *don't force it*.

> God is our refuge and strength,
>   an ever-present help in trouble.
> Therefore we will not fear, though the earth give way
>   and the mountains fall into the heart of the sea,
> though its waters roar and foam
>   and the mountains quake with their surging.
>
> (Ps. 46:1–3)

After I broke up with Jason, I felt pathetic for crying and talking constantly about my broken heart. I realize now that I needed those times of emotional chaos to help me get through my pain.

Allow yourself to break apart, and don't pretend it doesn't hurt. After the ties are finally severed, don't think you're an emotional freak if you flood the carpet with tears. It's psychologically healthy to fully mourn a loss. Don't beat yourself up for obsessing about your heartbreak, because each person deals with grief in a different way; process the grief as much or as long as you need to. Realize you'll eventually move on. It's true when people say, "It just takes time," and the unfortunate reality is, it may take a long time. Acknowledge that your despair stems from good qualities: you're probably loving, devoted, caring, and committed. When giving yourself entirely to a relationship, it would be unnatural if you didn't feel deeply grieved when it ends. Would you want to be so self-centered and uninvolved that you could easily set aside someone you adored? Feeling the way you do proves that you're normal and compassionate; it proves that *being a crybaby isn't so bad*. (See chapter 6 for the stages of grief.)

You need to persevere so that when you have done the will of God, you will receive what he has promised. (Heb. 10:36)

You were running superbly! Who cut in on you, deflecting you from the true course of obedience? This detour doesn't come from the One who called you into the race in the first place. (Gal. 5:7–8 MSG)

My hope is that you'll learn from my mistake: do not put off the breakup until tomorrow. Usually tomorrow turns into the next day, and it might eventually end in your walking down the aisle to say "I do" to someone who doesn't love the same God you do. Go to the bookstore and observe the ridiculous number of Christian support books written for women who find themselves linked to a nonbeliever "till death do them part." If you wait until tomorrow you'll only extend the pain for both you and him. By the end of that final conversation, be sure he knows you are no longer a couple. I once heard someone say, "Delayed obedience is disobedience," and I couldn't agree more. If you want to walk through new doors in life, it's necessary to close others behind you. That's why *closure is crucial*.

If you're reading this book, you probably already recognize that your romantic relationship is the detour mentioned in the quote from Galatians above. You realize you've been driving down a dead-end road, passing the blinking warning signs that have been trying to direct you down the right road. If you've made a serious decision to make Jesus the center of your life, and your boyfriend hasn't, you now know why it's time to break things off with the guy you love. There's nothing greater, nothing that can give you more relief than getting your life on track and gaining the freedom to follow God with all your heart. There's no relationship more fulfilling than a relationship with the Creator of the universe, and being in love can never compare to being in the will of God. You're about to discover the freedom such surrender brings.

After the split, you may experience overwhelming feelings of weakness. If you believe you're weak, you'll walk in weakness. The truth is, you're stronger than you imagine, because in our weakness the Lord is strong. Whatever you do, stay close to the Lord by talking, praying, or even screaming if you have to. Be honest with Him about your feelings.

I remember times in my car when I was driving with so many tears pouring down my face that they drenched the steering wheel as I cried out for comfort. In those vulnerable times I realized that I didn't have to be strong. The Bible says that we have His Spirit inside of us; the Creator of strength has offered to be strong for us. Ask Him to strengthen you, and He will. It's a simple request, but it doesn't mean you'll instantly feel strong. It takes some time to grieve as God works His hopes and plans within you. God cares about the details of your life, and He longs for you to be healed and to move forward.

Come fall on your knees with an open heart and believe that He is strong for you. "For everyone who asks, receives. Everyone who seeks, finds. And the door is opened to everyone who knocks" (Matt. 7:8 NLT).

When we're unsure of ourselves, we can be sure that the Lord has not given us a "spirit of fear" (2 Tim. 1:7 KJV). He is "the LORD, your God, who takes hold of your right hand and says to you, Do not fear; I will help you" (Isa. 41:13). He is pleased that you chose Him to be the priority in your life. He cannot and will not fail you. He thrives on showing you new discoveries as you venture down this newfound road. Allow Him to be in the driver's seat of your life, and He will lead you down the road of new life.

What If . . . ?

What If He's Interested in My Faith?

This can be exciting yet dangerous. If he's interested in knowing more about your faith, direct him to a church or a youth pastor who can share Christ with him. However, you need to pursue God separately until you can be sure he's truly interested. Make sure it's not a desperate attempt to prevent the breakup. I've heard countless stories of women who stayed with their guy because he was "open" to faith. Many come to discover that their boyfriends were only "open" to keep the relationship together. Because your emotions are heavily involved, it's important to have space, and if he's really interested in having a relationship with Christ, he needs time to get to know God on his own.

What If He Says He's a Christian Too?

The same rules apply. If you've already concluded that your relationship is pulling you farther away from God and His will for your life, you need to break up. Anyone can say, "I'm a Christian," but it's by the evidence of his or her life that you will know the truth. If there's no evidence of your guy pursuing God wholeheartedly, don't buy it.

What If He Becomes a Christian?

Beware of "conversions of convenience." Often, in order to date a girl, a guy will "make a commitment" to Jesus because he knows he has to in order to keep her. In fact, he may really try to get into it. However, if his decision isn't made from realizing his personal need for God, the "conversion" will be short-lived. Yet if he's sincere, let him prove his commitment on his own. Perhaps after several months you can start to pray about the possibility of reentering into a deeper relationship together. Problems may arise, however, if you're not patient enough to wait, and watch for his commitment.

What If I'm Experiencing Depression or Thoughts of Suicide?

Grief is a normal, healthy response to a breakup. Yet if you feel that you're slipping from ordinary grief into depression, or if you have thoughts of taking your own life, please tell someone you know or make an appointment with your doctor. If you don't feel comfortable talking about your feelings with someone you know, you can call a help line, such as 1-800-SUICIDE.

What If He Won't Stop Calling?

If he won't let up from pursuing you, make sure you've made your boundaries clear to him. If this doesn't work, be as firm as possible, explaining that you will not change your mind.

What If I'm Being Stalked?

If he won't stop showing up even after you've set your boundaries, or if he's following you or becoming obsessive, contact a parent or teacher, the police, or a stalking hotline.

Getting Through It, Not Over It

chapter six

Her breathing is heavy and labored. The inside of her head sounds like a cattle stampede. She trips and catches herself with her right hand. Her fingertips, caked with dirt, push her weight upright as she clutches her robe and runs for her life. Dust streams from her filthy hair and clothing, creating a cloud that obscures her lonely footprints behind her. Running, she views the scene she left behind as if in a nightmare playing repeatedly in her mind: family heirlooms, furniture, handmade clothes, her entire life swallowed in the flames that now burn her thoughts.

Tears blur her vision and trickle down to the edges of her cracked lips. Suddenly, she wails like a shofar piercing the air of the open plain. Her legs feel as if weighted with iron as she struggles to drag one in front of the other.

The last words she had heard echo in her mind, "Hurry! Whatever you do, do not look back."

The temptation to turn her head toward what she's just left behind pulls on her last bit of strength. *Just one last look to say good-bye.* A quick impulse, she whips her face around to look upon a city in flames. Dark strands of hair frame her eyes, matching the deepness of her widening pupils. There she stands, frozen in fear. The mortified woman watches as the angry fire and sulfur charge her, consuming her frame. Because she chose to gaze upon that which was behind, she perishes (see Gen. 19:15–26).

The angel of the Lord had commanded Lot and his family to flee Sodom and Gomorrah without looking back. It saddens me that Lot's wife looked back, but thinking about *why* she looked back breaks my heart. I believe she so dearly loved what she was leaving behind that she was willing to sacrifice everything, including her own life, for just one last look. The act of turning her head signified much more than just a "glance." She averted her eyes from the goal ahead because she'd left her heart behind her.

The story goes on: "The next morning Abraham was up early and hurried out to the place where he had stood in the LORD's presence. He looked out across the plains to Sodom and Gomorrah and saw columns of smoke and fumes, as from a furnace, rising from the cities there" (Gen. 19:27–28 NLT).

As Lot's wife raced across the desert plain she couldn't see the picture of God's plan to rescue her. She saw only what lay in front of her in the moment—a desert plain. She never chose to envision herself standing next to her husband, away from harm, victorious hands held high. She wasn't able to predict the tears of joy that would ultimately follow tears of pain.

I wonder what the outcome might have been had she obeyed God and kept her focus forward. I imagine her planted atop the mountain, her arms raised high, palms turned upward in praise, overflowing with gratitude to God for His faithfulness. Staring upward, she might have realized the things she had depended on came from dust, and to dust they had returned. Pillars of wood that once held up the roof of her house soon became kindling for the flame. Falling to her knees, she may have clung to the idea that nothing is permanent on earth. Truth would be brought into focus, and she would reflect upon how her heart had once been divided; her lesser love had been taken away.

I imagine Lot's wife taking in a breath of fresh air as she realized that, despite her doubt, God knew better. She had stood strong in obeying God when it hurt to do so, and as a result she received freedom from pain and the ability to see clearly.

Lot's wife will forever be known as "the disobedient woman who looked back when she was told not to." What an indescribable disappointment to have that reputation in print for eternity. Those two sentences in the Bible concerning Lot's wife seem insignificant, but they hold an enormous message about keeping God as our greatest love—even through pain and hardships.

If you're feeling torn between God and a guy, you may feel a little like Lot's wife. As you run toward God's plan, you may feel that you've left your heart back with the one you love. Even now you may be going through the motions of a breakup, yet your heart isn't in it; you know what you're "supposed to do" but temptation pulls hard. Like Lot's wife, you may be letting visions of what you're leaving behind take over your will to move forward in your relationship with God. The thought of losing someone you adore seems more painful than continuing to drag one foot in front of the other while staggering onward.

While breaking up should be quick and final, done in one giant step, letting go emotionally is really a process of smaller steps. Before my own breakup, I saw Lot's wife as a disobedient, brainless woman who didn't know what was best for her. After the breakup I found myself looking at her with compassion and understanding. I now believe that the story of Lot's wife's runs parallel to many of today's breakup stories.

Don't beat yourself up if you're feeling a pull to "look back." As you focus forward, you will eventually heal. The more we look back, the greater the pain. The more we look ahead, the larger our hope becomes. When your mind is telling you to get over it, focus on just getting through it by putting one foot in front of the other.

However, we must have faith that the Lord can gratify the desires of our hearts better than we ever will be able to (see Ps. 37:4). At times you may wish to turn back toward your previous relationship as Lot's wife turned back to her city . . . her home. Be honest with God and voice to Him how you feel; realize it's impossible to shock Him with your thoughts. I remember feeling guilty for repeatedly wanting to run back to Jason after our breakup. I prayed, "Lord, I don't know who I love more, You or him. I'm so sorry. I don't know why You still want me when I don't even know if I want You."

When I finally took the leap to be honest with God, He showed me something I'll never forget: I don't always have to know what I want; I only need to trust Him for what He wants for me. "Trust in the LORD with all your heart; do not depend on your own understanding. Seek his will in all you do, and he will direct your paths" (Prov. 3:5–6 NLT).

God knows what's best for us. He knew Lot's wife would be most fulfilled when in His presence, safe from harm on the mountain. He also knows we will be most fulfilled when with Him. He sees aspects of our hearts that we cannot see. He can name desires that we haven't yet desired. Because God created us in such a way that only He can fulfill us, we will encounter peace only if we stay close to Him. When we reach the end of the dry plains (our pain and doubt) and arrive at the top of the mountain (peace and trust), we'll understand in new ways that God is good in what He commands and provides.

But first we must let go of what is pulling us away from God. The dreaded words "letting go" flow against the tide of our modern-day society. We're supposed to be strong and in control of our lives. Jesus said,

> Anyone who intends to come with me has to let me lead. You're not in the driver's seat—I am. Don't run from suffering; embrace it. Follow me and I'll show you how. Self-help is no help at all.

Self-sacrifice is the way, my way, to finding yourself, your true self. What good would it do to get
everything you want and lose you, the real you?
(Luke 9:23–25 MSG)

One summer not long after my breakup, I led a group of girls
through Young Life at a popular Christian camp in Canada.
Young Life is a Christ-based organization that allows youth lead-
ers to build relationships with teenagers in public high schools
throughout the United States. As a leader, I thought I was supposed to have it all together, yet I felt anything but stable. Our
speaker of the week offered to pray for any campers who were
having a difficult time letting God take over their lives; I was the
first to go forward.

Until this point I'd felt like Lot's wife: running with blurred
vision on a dry plain, unable to stop choking on the dust, and vir-
tually consumed by an urge to look back. I was tired, and it was
my time to cry for help.

Holding an armful of heavy books, I explained to a nice older
woman that I'd been having a hard time letting go of my ex-
boyfriend. Despite him not understanding my faith, I still loved
him. As I continued speaking, I expected her to gently lay her
hands on me and pray. However, in the middle of my sentence she
ripped the books out of my arms, lifted them high over her head,
and with a huge thud, let them land in front of my feet. I stood
speechless, shocked at what she'd done. I stared at her wide-eyed
and waited for an explanation. *Weren't prayer people supposed to be
gentle and sweet?*

Before I could say anything she instructed, "Drop it like a
rock!"

A little embarrassed because everyone suddenly stared at me, I
leaned in and quietly asked, "Huh?"

"You cannot hold on to this relationship anymore! It's not
about how you feel; it's a choice. You have to drop it violently;
you cannot slowly lower it down. Run and don't look back."

This isn't what I wanted to hear. I wanted someone to help me with my *feelings*. I wanted someone who would weep when I wept.

When you feel too exhausted to go on, it's important to reach out to someone who can see the whole picture even though you can't. We can become enveloped in a cloud of emotions and our view of truth may be obscured. Often we can't get past our current pain, but others may be able to see more clearly and help focus our vision toward God.

What might have happened if the angel of the Lord had said to Lot's family, "Well, I guess you can run . . . or maybe walk or jog . . . just make sure you get out of the city . . . sometime . . . whenever." God foreknew that His people would be destroyed if they didn't run.

The act of letting go of your ex is a choice, just as Lot's family had a choice to run. If we sit and wait for the moment when it suddenly *feels right* to let go, it may never happen. If we lived our lives fueled first by feelings, many of us would eat chocolate all day, tell our boss what we really think of her, and probably have no friends.

When our emotions take over, we have to remember and remind ourselves of the truth. Pick up your Bible and pray to truly believe what it says. I'm sure Lot and his family didn't feel like leaving the city. Yet they knew they had to because it concerned their safety. When you have an urge to call your ex-boyfriend, run the other way. In times of feeling lonely, know that you are never alone. "The LORD keeps watch over you as you come and go, both now and forever" (Ps. 121:8 NLT). When thoughts of life coming to an end fill your mind, know that God gives you hope and a future in this world (Jer. 29:11).

Letting go is a conscious choice. Drop it, walk away, and don't look back.

You might feel like you're never going to get your heart back. Aspects of everyday life trigger memories of your past relationship, and then what? Remember that you don't have to get *over it* in order to get *through it*. Your feeling of attachment is going to eventually work itself through. The depth and intensity of your relationship will determine how long it may take to move on; until then you can work toward getting through it. A desire for the guy will leave when a truly greater desire takes his place.

> I am still not all I should be, but I am focusing all my energies on this one thing: Forgetting the past and looking forward to what lies ahead, I strain to reach the end of the race and receive the prize for which God, through Christ Jesus, is calling us up to heaven. (Phil. 3:13–14 NLT)

You get your heart back by making Christ the greatest desire of your heart. We've already established that our ultimate fulfillment will come through knowing Christ more. As the verse above says, focus all of your energy on knowing Him more. As you spend time with the Lord, He will reveal Himself to you, and it's inevitable that you'll fall more in love with Him. As you lose focus of what you're walking away from, your heart will no longer belong to what lies behind. When you spend time conversing with God and reading His words to you, He will shape your desires to resemble His own. Soon you'll have your heart back.

Those things or people that we most focus our energies on are usually the priority of our lives. If you focus on knowing the Lord, He will naturally enter into the forefront of your life. As you graduate toward deeper intimacy with Him, your broken heart will start to heal while you bask in Christ's love. If you focus on doing things that lift you up and help you grow, the things that pulled you back will seem less important.

Get involved with something that utilizes the gifts God gave to you. Your local church is a good first choice, and then you can branch into other areas of involvement as well. I got involved with an organization called Young Life that not only put my talents to good use, it surrounded me with friends and kept me accountable to stay on track.

Something that might cause you to "look back" is that most women are born nurturers. We need to be needed. I remember being haunted by the thought, *What will Jason do without me? If I'm not there for him when he needs me, I'm a horrible person, and as a result he may not survive!* This is a lie. If you're feeling the same way you must stop now! Realize that you're not ultimately responsible for the well being of another human being—God is. Making myself responsible for Jason's well being was not only dragging me down, it was actually arrogant.

One of the most intimate aspects of love is trust. Do you trust God enough to hand over your relationship to Him? Surrendering Jason to the Lord's hands was one of the hardest things I've ever had to do. It meant that I not only let go of our relationship, but I let go of control. I had to trust that God was sovereign enough, loving enough, and good enough to hold someone I adored.

Things would have turned out differently if Lot's wife hadn't depended on her own understanding (see Prov. 3:5 NLT). Instead, she held tightly to her own ideas of what was best for her future. The Lord longs to take us from our vast desert to the mountain-top, where He can stand beside us. When we stand in the place God has planned for us, we can at last see clearly because our main focus is not on our circumstances but on the Giver of peace. God sees from the beginning to the end. He is always leading us to a higher place, a place of safety and peace where our souls were designed to rest.

Try this exercise as a way to process letting go. Imagine that you're holding the person you love in a tight fist. Take a deep breath and reach your arms forward to the One who loves this person far deeper than you can ever imagine. Slowly begin to relax your fingers. Loosening your grip will change you. It will bring freedom into your life. Recognize that it's impossible for you to love your guy more that God does. Still uncurling your fingers from that white-knuckled grip, look away as God the Father, the One who knows everything, the Creator of roaring seas and endless skies, the Lover of our souls, gently scoops your guy from your care. The Lord holds the one you love while look-ing at him with unconditional love. Watch as God cradles him with more care than you're capable of giving. Step back and re-alize the Lord loved him before you did. Understand that your love was but an extension of the endless affection God feels for him. Your connection to your boyfriend should now be only through prayer. Talking to God on your boyfriend's behalf may be the stepping-stone that allows him to enter into a relation-ship with God. Beyond anything and everything, be assured that you've left him in the hands of Someone who understands the love you feel for him. He understands the love to such depth that He gave His life for him.

We can learn from Lot's wife, who made an irreversible deci-sion. Trek through the tiresome, dusty plains so you can arrive at the mountain. Don't look back; keep your eyes on the Lord, and soon you'll lift your hands high in thankfulness.

Getting Through the Desert Days

The process of letting go is a lot like the grieving process (see below). Remember, it's entirely normal to grieve when experiencing a great loss; give yourself plenty of room to mourn. At the same time, though, recognize that there's no promised day of total wellness. Assess your place in the grieving process so you understand where you are and know what to expect in the days ahead. People go through these stages in different orders and to varying degrees. The process requires patience and time, but most people experience some or all of the steps:

1. *Denial.* Denial is generally the first stage in the grieving process. It can be experienced as numbness, avoidance, isolation, or direct denial. In this stage, we can't believe the loss is true. We may tell ourselves that it didn't really happen. It doesn't seem real.

2. *Anger.* Another stage of grief is anger. At this point, we've gotten past some or all of the denial, but now we're angry about the loss. We may want to take it out on something or someone, or we may just express our anger in ways that are familiar to us.

3. *Bargaining.* In the bargaining stage, we're trying to come up with ways to retrieve what was lost, or find someone or something to blame. Common thoughts include "If only I'd just . . ." or "I wish we could have . . ." or "Maybe if I do this . . ." In the case of lost relationships, we may actually

bargain with the people we lost—or with God—in an effort to get them back: "If I change my behavior, will you come back?"

4. *Depression*. The depression stage is a time of profound sadness. It generally follows denial, anger, and bargaining when we feel helpless and hopeless to stop the loss. It may include crying, withdrawal, and a number of other things that express sadness.

5. *Acceptance*. The final stage is acceptance. Most often we've traveled through all of the above stages (oftentimes more than once) before getting to acceptance. At this stage we have to some extent reorganized ourselves and our thinking to incorporate the loss. This doesn't mean we no longer mourn the loss from time to time, but the sadness is now a part of us and doesn't keep us from functioning normally. Over time the intensity of the sadness generally diminishes, yet it may never entirely leave us.

Recognizing these stages can develop your empathy and support for others while providing permission for you to walk through this process in your own way and in your own time.

Who Am I Without You?
chapter seven

The older I become the more I see myself as a broken human rather than a spiritual pillar. If I told you all of the disgusting thoughts I have in a day you probably wouldn't want to sit at the same lunch table with me. I'll confess a few. I felt convicted to send one hundred dollars to missionaries; instead I spent one hundred and twenty on a new pair of rhinestone-trimmed jeans. I regularly size myself up against others, and if I end up on the lower scale, I search for their flaws until I'm satisfied. Gossip is my drug, and in the moment, it's fun to slander someone, yet afterward I feel disgusting. I purposely exaggerate to make myself sound interesting. I believe that I'm right about all of my opinions. This is but the fringe of the person I am on the inside.

A few years ago, my two roommates and I packed everything we owned into a two-door Honda and a 1985 Corolla. We were moving to Orange County, California, with hopes of new adventure and an exciting future. As we approached the desert, the air conditioning went out in the car we were riding in. Despite delirium from the heat, laughter, and our sweaty bodies . . . we felt alive! Single, adventurous, and free, we were on a mission to conquer the world . . . but more specifically, Orange County.

Oh, how naive we were. The first few months of roaming Laguna Beach were so shocking that I might as well have been a cave woman imported to the heart of New York City. The shiny Beamers looked like an empty substitute for satisfaction. This is a city where bottles of hair bleach are emptied as often as water bottles. I thought I was different: *I'm not one of them; I'm not shallow. I'm confident, and I don't have image issues.*

Jason and I had broken up years ago, and I was deep into writing this book. I was arrogant enough to believe that I would have a revolutionary effect on this town. I soon learned the reality: we're all made from the same stuff. We're prone to the same sins . . . some of us more than others. If poison lingers in the air, it will seep into the blood, and soon I became concerned about appearance. The more I was concerned with who I was in the mirror, the faster the inside of me crumbled. I soon noticed that my chest was small . . . I never cared before. *A few highlights might brighten my face,* I thought. My Corolla became an embarrassment rather than a blessing. The competition for men was steep. If I wanted a guy, especially a Christian guy, I had to step it up. For every somewhat attractive Christian guy, there were twenty-five blondes flouncing around with Bibles in hand.

I definitely was headed for an identity crisis. Our identity is, after all, a collection of many different elements. My worth has always been at the mercy of whomever I thought I was in love with at the moment. I've always been boy crazy. In fact, when I was in seventh grade my parents ripped me out of the public school for a year because my obsession with boys was causing my grades to plummet. I felt gloriously alive when a guy showed me attention because I thought this attention proved my beauty and desirability.

For many of us, this continual hunt for identity is a tiresome battle. We allow boyfriends, family, media, and our society to tell us who we should be. In the book *Captivating*, Stasi Eldredge says, "Every woman I've ever met feels it—something deeper than just the sense of failing at what she does. An underlying, gut feeling of failing at who she *is*, I *am not enough*, and, *I am too much* at the same time."[1]

So who are we without our guys? We break up and suddenly realize we've spent so much time focusing on him and the relationship, that the inside of us has become invisible. I used to stand in front of the mirror, pulling shirts off over my head and throwing them in a "discard-because-Jason-might-not-like-it" pile. My name was no longer *Stina*, it was *Jasonandstina*. If we were apart, the first question someone would ask was "Where's Jason?" I started to feel that I wasn't my own person if he wasn't attached to my hip. If I wasn't accepted by him, I didn't feel accepted. If we disagreed, my world turned into a gray haze. I didn't know who I was, what I wanted, what I believed, or what I was doing on earth. I allowed Jason to answer all of my unknowns, and soon, I willingly became but an extension of my boyfriend.

Before moving to California from Seattle, my roommate Erika and I used to dedicate a whole day every week to discussing our problems; we named it "Sundays with Eri." After discussing the sermon from that morning we always intended to go up to our apartment, but instead we usually wound up drenched with tears, in a parked car next to our building overlooking Lake Union. Each Sunday we felt exhausted yet revived, believing that we'd solved yet another complex part of ourselves by digging up ugly rotting roots. Our issues usually included questioning God, boyfriends, or our relationships with our parents.

As much as I loved these bonding moments with Erika, I soon felt that Jesus was challenging me to bring my confusion to Him. Discussing our problems with friends is helpful, but ultimately we need to discuss them with Jesus first and let Him begin the change that needs to happen in our lives. Nothing can heal like Jesus can, but it takes a certain amount of bravery to come to Jesus, because when we do, we won't be able to escape the change that comes along with it. And change is seldom comfortable.

Whatever issues, big or small, are buried within, Jesus is willing to go there. He has been healing deep wounds since He walked the earth. In Mark chapter 5, Jesus arrives at a new town and finds a man cutting himself and mumbling craziness. This man was an outcast. We all have them in our towns. It's that person mumbling on the street corner, or the crazy uncle whom you speak about in a hushed, rushed, glad-I'm-not-him tone of voice.

When Jesus came upon this crazy man, He asked the man his name. Jesus, of course, knew his name, yet maybe He was curious to know how the *man* identified himself. The man answered, "My name is Legion because there are many." The man did not identify himself by his born name. He identified himself by his problem—he was possessed by a legion of demons (a *legion* is a large number or multitude of something).

We often identify ourselves and others in the same way. What personal struggle has become your identity? Without even knowing it, some people inflict themselves with the labels of weak, unlovable, mistake maker, slut, weird, partier, or [enter name here]'s girlfriend. An identity can be a label that someone else has attached to you: mistake, disappointment, undeserving.

Jesus had a heart to heal the demon-possessed man and at the same time wash away the lies and the self-inflicted name-calling. Christ wants to restore you. He wants you to be what He intended you to be before sin entered the world and broke things. "'But I will restore you to health and heal your wounds,' declares the Lord" (Jer. 30:17).

If we identify ourselves by our problems, we're *accepting* a confused self. After my breakup I believed I was a mess that needed to be fixed. I sometimes think of myself as being like my grandma's rocking chair. When she first got it as a gift, it was in perfect condition, shiny and smelling of rich mahogany. Because it has aged and become scratched doesn't mean it's worthless; it just needs time, love, and care to bring it back to its original state. So we take it out to the garage with a vision in mind. After some sanding and staining we stand back with pride, because we knew it had beautiful potential all along. God wants to restore us, to bring us back to our original state according to His design. When we submit ourselves to God's work, He swoops in and restores us.

The book of Romans questions, "Don't you realize that whatever you choose to obey becomes your master? You can choose sin, which leads to death, or you can choose to obey God and receive his approval" (6:16 NLT). If you become a slave to something or someone, you have yourself to blame, because somewhere in your life, you voluntarily yielded yourself to that "thing." Similarly, if you choose to obey God it's because you yielded yourself to Him. Whoever or whatever you allow to master you will take ownership of your identity, and you will accept it as true.

According to the dictionary, a slave is someone regarded as the property of the person he or she works for, or it is a person who is completely dominated by someone or something. So who are *you* working for? What owns you, and is it someone or something that will give you a trustworthy assessment? What *thing* in your life dominates you? It's time we claim *Jesus Christ* as our master, and base our identity on who He tells us we are.

When Jesus asks you your name, maybe you don't answer "John's girlfriend." Perhaps, though, you've lost sight of who you are as a child of the Most High. Possibly you were never told in the first place. But there's a part in all of us that secretly cries, "Who am I?"

If your identity was previously and totally wrapped up in your boyfriend, his absence is likely causing those thick layers of personal definition to start sloughing off. You may find yourself alone and clueless: "Who am I now?" Being alone, though, may force us to rediscover our passions, talents, pet peeves, dreams, and abilities—in all their fullness through Christ.

We need to find our identity in Christ, not in the people and circumstances around us. "Finding your identity in Christ" is a slogan that sounds unattainably spiritual, but rather than allow the phrase to float over our heads, let's grab hold of it, tear it apart, understand it, and allow it to become the foundation of "Who am I?"

God is ready to show you who you are to Him. Being single is precious because it can provide a sanctuary for God to speak clearly to you. He wants to tell you, "I love you. Now let Me reveal your identity, plan, purpose, worth, and, most importantly, My unconditional and passionate love for you." This time can be incredibly vital to your future. In fact, this time with your Creator could actually save your future marriage, if that's what God has in mind for you.

We discover who we really are when we're wrapped up in the arms of the One who created us. There are countless Scripture passages telling us Who it is we belong to, who we are, and how God sees us. Below is just a sampling of the wealth of encouragement found in the Bible. When you feel you've lost sight of who you are, read the verses below aloud to yourself, putting your name in the spaces.

If [your name] is in Christ, [she] is a new creation; the old has gone, the new has come! (2 Cor. 5:17)

But now he has reconciled [your name] by Christ's physical body through death to present you holy in his sight, without blemish and free from accusation. (Col. 1:22)

How great is the love the Father has lavished on [your name], that [she] should be called [a child] of God! And that is what [you] are! (1 John 3:1)

Praise be to the God and Father of our Lord Jesus Christ, who has blessed [you] in the heavenly realms with every spiritual blessing in Christ. For he chose [your name] in him before the creation of the world to be holy and blameless in his sight. In love he predestined [you] to be adopted as his [daughter] though Jesus Christ, in accordance with his pleasure and will—to the praise of his glorious grace, which he has freely given [you] in the One he loves. In him [you] have redemption through his blood, the forgiveness of sins, in accordance with the riches of God's grace that he lavished on [you] with all wisdom and understanding. (Eph. 1:3–8)

There is now no condemnation for [your name] who [is] in Christ Jesus. (Rom. 8:1)

My sheep listen to my voice; I know them, and they follow me. I give them eternal life, and they shall never perish; no one can snatch them out of my hand. (John 10:27–28)

Neither death nor life, neither angels nor demons, neither the present nor the future, nor any powers, neither height nor depth, nor anything else in all creation, will be able to separate [your name] from the love of God that is in Christ Jesus our Lord. (Rom. 8:38–39)

God has said,

> "Never will I leave [your name];
>   never will I forsake you."

So [you] say with confidence,

> "The Lord is my helper; I will not be afraid.
>   What can man do to me?"

(Heb. 13:5–6)

And surely I am with you always, to the very end of the age. (Matt. 28:20)

Even the very hairs of [your name] head are all numbered [by God]. (Matt. 10:30)

If by the Spirit you put to death the misdeeds of the body, you will live, because those who are led by the Spirit of God are sons of God. For you did not receive a spirit that makes you a slave again to fear, but you received a Spirit of sonship. And by him [you] cry, "Abba, Father." The Spirit himself testifies with [your] spirit that [you] are God's [child]. Now if [you] are [a child], then [you] are [an heir—an heir] of God and [a coheir] with Christ, if indeed [you] share in his sufferings in order that [you] may also share in his glory. (Rom. 8:13–17)

This is the confidence [your name] [has] in approaching God: that if [you] ask anything according to his will, he hears [you]. And if [you] know that he hears [you]—whatever [you] ask— [you] know that [you] have what [you] asked of him. (1 John 5:14–15)

[Your name,] when you pass through the waters,
    I will be with you;
and when you pass through the rivers,
    they will not sweep over you.
When you walk through the fire,
    you will not be burned;
      the flames will not set you ablaze.

                        (Isa. 43:2)

The Lord your God is with you,
    he is mighty to save.

He will take great delight in you,
  he will quiet you with his love,
  he will rejoice over you with singing.

(Zeph. 3:17)

[Your name,] you are [part of] a chosen people, a royal priesthood, a holy nation, a people belonging to God, that you may declare the praises of him who called you out of darkness into his wonderful light. (1 Peter 2:9)

The one who is in you is greater than the one who is in the world. (1 John 4:4)

The Spirit helps [you] in [your] weakness. [You] do not know what [you] ought to pray for, but the Spirit himself intercedes for [you] with groans that words cannot express. And he who searches [your heart] knows the mind of the Spirit, because the Spirit intercedes for the saints in accordance with God's will. And [you] know that in all things God works for the good of those who love him, who have been called according to his purpose. (Rom. 8:26–28)

I can do everything through him who gives me strength. (Phil. 4:13)

Whatever happens, conduct [yourself] in a manner worthy of the gospel of Christ. (Phil. 1:27)

What is in us that strives for perfection, when the Bible screams loud and clear that we'll never be flawless on Earth? We need Christ to fill in our inadequacies. This need came to me recently when I realized that so many of my weaknesses can't be kept to myself. It seems that a lot of my weaknesses have been broadcast on a stage under a bright spotlight. I get in a car accident at least once every six months, and actually I backed into a Hyundai this afternoon and crunched the bumper. I lose my keys at least once a day. My room is always a mess, and a landlord told me, "It looks like a bunch of druggies live in your room." My bills are late nearly every month. I just vacuumed the piles of sand in my car from months of accumulation in the corners of my floor mats. I still have two chapters in this book to write to complete by a deadline, and instead of writing, I decide to check MySpace. I'm not organized, and feel like giving up on details. I get really down on myself and sometimes wonder if God became accidentally distracted when He created my brain.

Recently I sat at the end of a long, intimidating table, facing the regional director of a huge real estate firm. She was interviewing me to be her assistant. She told me she was looking for someone with a "keen eye for detail," someone who is very organized and loves to work behind the scenes with numbers and computers. My heart clenched and my mouth dried out. I envisioned myself answering phones and writing schedules—and it looked like a prison sentence. With a big plastic smile, my lips motioned how I would like the job, but my heart screamed . . . Ruuuuuuuuun!

The moment I walked out of that office, though, was the moment I stopped hating myself for lacking in certain areas. I began embracing the fact that God made me—weaknesses and all—for His purposes. I may not be a moneymaker, a number-adder, a clothes-folder, or a paper-filer, but I am a speaker, a passionate writer, a people lover, an adventuress, and a pioneer. Our weaknesses only serve to showcase our greatest strengths. My lack of organization makes it comfortable for me to be chaotic and entertaining with girls in high school ministry. Deciding against a business career has allowed me time to write and live out my personal passion.

Discover and embrace your true personality. More than likely, the things that annoy you most about yourself are the very things that enable you to be who God created you to be.

God sees you as an individual. Please stop and think about this for a minute. When I picture myself, I subconsciously envision my imperfect self among a sea of other faces, all with perfect lives. Yet when God looks at us, He sees past the issues, the insecurities, and the worn-down interiors. He sees us up close; He hears each beat of our hearts and knows what they long for. He hears the thoughts we haven't yet uttered, and He is here.

We need to look at ourselves as individuals and not compare ourselves to others. Start learning how to see yourself compared to *you*. Of course we'll always have certain insecurities, yet healing begins with tiny steps. When God was forming you in the womb, He wasn't manipulating your personality so you could someday become the perfect puzzle piece to fit your boyfriend. He was thinking how your beautiful existence would bring glory to His name.

> We are confident of all this because of our great trust in God through Christ. It is not that we think we can do anything of lasting value by ourselves. Our only power and success come from God. (2 Cor. 3:4–5 NLT)

Who I am is enough. I don't have to strive to be like the masses surrounding me, because God made me to be an individual with my unique talents, passions, weird quirks, and sometimes irritating weaknesses. I am enough. I am His masterpiece. I am complete with or without a boyfriend. A masterpiece wouldn't be a masterpiece if there were two Mona Lisas, two Sistine Chapels, or two Beethoven's Fifth Symphonies. And a masterpiece wouldn't be a masterpiece if the Mona Lisa looked more like the Sistine Chapel. You are the only one of your type. You are your own breed. You fill a place in this world that no one else can fill. And the God who created the masterpiece called you, and stands back in admiration of His handiwork.

We can do nothing of lasting value, though, on our own. Paintings do not paint themselves; the artist gets ultimate glory and credit. Sometimes people stop and stare and admire the art-work, but at the end of the day, it's the artist who has created the masterpiece.

Take this time of singleness to uncover the hidden parts of what makes you *you*. Ask God why He created you. Allow your time with Him to become the cornerstone of the woman He is form-ing you into. Let yourself be who you are right now, weaknesses and strengths. Step from away from the person you want to be in other people's eyes and step into the truth.

Taking a Detour

chapter eight

Dear God,

> Oh God, how far I have fallen.
> My eyes are so puddled with tears
> that I can no longer see You.
> Are You there?
> I know Your plan is truth,
> and yet my sins take over my youth.
> I judge prostitutes and all the while
> I willingly do it for free . . .
> how many times must I fall before
> You turn Your back on me?
> I'm so sorry.

"We're all sluts on the inside," my coworker said with a mischievous grin. I immediately knew what she meant. Christian or not, we all have temptations. We have a tendency in us that leans away from God. Our hearts beg us to do what is right, but our flesh wants the opposite. My coworker called it being a "slut." The Bible tells us we are slaves to our own sin.

> I don't understand myself at all, for I really want to do what is right, but I don't do it. Instead, I do the very thing I hate. I know perfectly well that what I am doing is wrong, and my bad conscience shows that I agree that the law is good. But I can't help myself, because it is sin inside me that makes me do these evil things. (Rom. 7:15–17 NLT)

This conversation with my coworker was in my mind one day when I flipped on the TV and saw Christina Aguilera doing a special on sex education in schools. She investigated two different methods: the safe-sex program (handing out condoms in schools) and the abstinence programs (comprised mainly of Christians). As I observed both sides of the spectrum, something struck me as not quite right. It seemed that abstinence is unrealistic for those who don't know God's plan for their lives, yet handing out condoms is too much like encouraging kids to have sex. I thought, *If young people are going to abstain, they need motivation that goes beyond disease prevention.*

If you're reading this book, I assume you have a relationship with God and are seeking His will for your life. You've probably heard a near infinite number of reasons to wait for sex, but you may be thinking, *What if it's too late?* After my breakup, no matter what anyone told me about forgiveness, I felt dirtier than my virgin friends. I convinced myself I was the runt of God's litter. To my mind, I'd be the last one to get a prayer answered, and I'd have to work hard to make up for my unwise choices. I knew God could forgive, but how could He forget?

After years of convincing myself that I was over Jason, that he was over me, and it was God's will that we should never speak, see, or touch again, I found myself in a hot tub with his T-shirt twisted around my body. He slid his hands around my waist, tightened his grip, and pulled me close.

I didn't intend to end up there. My first thought when I woke up that morning was not, "Hmm . . . I'm going to hang out with Jason, and I think I might spend the night in his bed." No, the encounter started out like a misty rain and became a downpour. I wasn't paying attention. I wasn't praying. I allowed myself to be pulled by the riptides of temptation, and it sucked me in over my head.

The Bible says, "The heart is deceitful above all things, and desperately wicked: who can know it?" (Jer. 17:9 KJV).

Because I wasn't prepared, I fell neck deep into a situation where I lost control. My heart spun, and the warm invitation of familiarity beckoned. The practical side of me cringed while another part of me was thrilled to spit this in God's face: I wanted to say, "You can take him away from me but I'll always love him. Look what my broken heart caused me to do!" It felt like my insides were collapsing as I turned my face to Jason's. I thought, *How did I get here? Is this really happening?* We broke up almost a decade ago, and now we were acting like he'd just come back from war. I knew that later there would be emotional consequences, but in that moment I didn't care.

At six AM the next morning, I walked to my car. The jingling of my key chain added to my anxiety as my head hung low. I looked down and couldn't believe that these same feet that had just slipped from Jason's bed could stand in front of teenage girls while I proclaimed a message I was incapable of living. I rested my head on top of the car and debated whether Jason and I should get back together. The thought of my "old life" was somehow strangely comforting—no more struggling to do what God asked and no more unknowns. Being barefoot and pregnant sounded infinitely more appealing than suppressing my feelings for Jason for the rest of my life.

As I drove home, the yellow traffic lines blurred into squiggles as I wept. Stepping back from the situation I asked myself, *Why am I feeling this resentment toward God? Am I crazy, lonely, or furious?*

How did a friendly phone call end with us being naked, staring at his ceiling? Fear flooded my heart. *Here I am, right where I began. But now, where do I go from here?*

I didn't realize I was mad and resentful at God until I had rested in Jason's arms the night before. *He is selfish to take Jason away because He wants me all to Himself.* I was livid that God's desires had caused me to suffer all these years. It crossed my mind that the sacrifice it took to be in "God's will" was a price I could not afford. I wanted to give up and blame my mistake on God's selfishness.

I came home and read over the first few chapters of this book, as yet unpublished. I secretly hoped that my words were all a fabrication I created to convince myself I was better off without Jason. Did our breakup prematurely end a high school relationship, or was it really something I had to do so that I could grow spiritually? I desperately searched for an answer that could assure me I'd be okay if we reunited. *I could be patient. Love is patient, right?* Yet I felt I deserved punishment. *I already messed up sexually, so why not just keep doing it?*

I skimmed over my own words, searching for a glitch or a lie. But despite the whispers of my deceitful heart, each sentence comforted me and once again solidified the truth that God's way was the right way. The truth always remains the same despite our inability to live it out, and truth forced me to ask myself these sobering questions:

1. Who would I pray with?
2. Who would pray for my children?
3. Do I want to sit in church alone for the rest of my life?
4. Could I really live with tape over my lips when everything in me wanted to scream the greatness of God?
5. How could I minister to others, being married to someone who didn't understand my motive for ministry?

The tears came as I realized how the Lord loved me first, and it is *my choice* to love Him back. God's love for me was so all-consuming that it drew me to Him. I was reminded that, at the core, my relationship with Christ took priority over any boy. I couldn't deny it no matter how much I missed Jason. It was *my choice* to prevent any human relationship (passionate or not) to dull this ongoing romance with my Creator. God did not force me to do anything. It was His love that consumed me, and in response I could offer nothing less than all of me.

Still, I have trouble getting this whole purity thing right. Before Jason, I'd always been unwavering about not having sex before marriage. I was obstinate about being abstinent . . . until the opportunity arose to have sex. It didn't take much to abandon my vow of virginity—just a few butterflies, some sweet words, and the awakening bliss of being touched.

I'd been adamant about not having sex before I was married, but only because it's what my parents had taught me to believe, even though they themselves had not waited. They believed it was best because it's what their parents had taught them, even though their parents had not followed through either. Waiting for the wedding night just sounded good and safe. I thought it was what God heavily suggested *somewhere* in the Bible.

After I'd given my life to Jesus, though, every time I had sex I felt an intense emptiness. Why was that? I felt ashamed and disgusted with myself for giving in, yet could never explain the reason why. I felt separated from God, and void of His love. The impulsive desire to instantly gratify my sexual longings sometimes overpowered my love for God, and the more I tried to justify my lack of control, the more I knew I had a choice: Him or him.

Even long after I had broken up with Jason, my decision to follow God's desire for purity was put to the test. I had a hard time, though, relating to Christian books on premarital sex because the writers seemed to say that after their sexual experiences, they felt like a piece of meat—used and abused. But I hadn't felt that way; having sex was, after all, my decision. Furthermore, a lot of messages I heard seemed to say, "Your life hasn't ended if you've been in a sexual relationship. There is hope for your future!" But I hadn't felt guilt and remorse over a premarital relationship, and this only made me think that there was something wrong with me. Maybe my sexual past had spiritually stunted me forever.

Then one Monday morning, something made me begin to think that I could get back on my feet once again. It happened on Talia Street. My neighbors on Talia Street have little in common besides the name of our street. The family to the right of my house are good people. They're white, middle-class Americans in their early fifties. They garden every Sunday. They always have pleasant smiles and enjoy local neighbor kids who come to help dig in the garden. My neighbors on the left side are going through a divorce. Rumor has it that she left him for another man. The soon-to-be ex-husband is a quiet guy, and his soon-to-be ex-wife occasionally shows up at the house to take a dresser or say hi to the kids. A family just moved in three houses down; they came from Africa to be missionaries to our neighborhood.

I thought about these three families one Monday morning, because Monday is when we walk to the end of our driveways to do the same thing. It struck me that despite our differing backgrounds, family dynamics, hobbies, and beliefs, everyone who lives on Talia Street takes the garbage out on Monday.

It doesn't matter who we are or where we live, each one of us has garbage in our lives that needs to be taken out. This junk needs to be brought before God, as we allow Him to throw it "as far as the east is from the west" (Ps. 103:12).

In a way, Jesus is like a garbage man: He came so that we can have freedom from our "dirtiness." He died on the cross so that we can put all our garbage on Him, and He can throw it away. "For God did not send his Son into the world to condemn the world, but to save the world through him" (John 3:17).

Before we take out the garbage of our lives, we have to ask God for forgiveness. But there's a difference between just saying "sorry" and repentance. Weak apologies are pure lip service; repentance is an action. Repentance means you hate the sin. It's turning around and facing an opposite direction. *Sorry* is a worthless word unless the heart is broken and repentant.

I used to think that if I squeezed my eyes shut and thought hard enough about how gross my sin was, then I might feel guilty for it. But I admit there were times I simply didn't feel guilty for what I had done sexually. We cannot muster up repentance; it is through an authentic relationship with Christ that His Spirit convicts us, washes us, and takes away the shame. As we draw closer to the Lord, we draw "super"-naturally away from our sinful nature.

As the Spirit convicts, the weight of sin can be backbreaking. How do we repent without carrying away the overwhelming burden of condemnation? Somehow, we don't feel condemned every Monday when we take our stinky garbage out to the curb, but when it comes to taking our stinky garbage before God, we do. We're giving our garbage to a pure, holy, and most loving God.

This self-condemnation is one of the biggest things that prevents us from getting closer to Christ. Yet the Bible says we can be confident when we come before God. Because Jesus has provided access for us, we can come boldly to the throne of grace. No sin is too large or unspeakable to lay before the cross. If we think it is, we're proclaiming that His sacrifice of death and His resurrection is not enough. Forgiving others is tough, but forgiving ourselves is the most difficult task. "It is by our actions that we know we are living in the truth, so we will be confident when we stand before the Lord, even if our hearts condemn us. For God is greater than our hearts, and he knows everything" (1 John 3:19–20 NLT).

It's taken me a lot of time to convince myself that I'm not "damaged goods." People tried to tell me I was forgiven but until the Lord sealed it in my heart, it wasn't real. One day I went for a walk with one of my wisest friends, Stephanie. I was feeling so much condemnation, and I was having a hard time looking her in the eyes as we talked. I couldn't handle hiding my secret life anymore. I burst into tears and confessed it all. She calmly placed her hand on my arm, looked me straight in the eyes and said, "Stina, keeping your virginity doesn't make you whole; God does. You know that, right?"

Those words reached a part of my heart that hadn't been touched before—the part that was hardened and full of shame. I realized I'd been looking to people, rules, and my behavior to guarantee wholeness when God was saying, "*I* make you whole."

Trouble is, this wholeness isn't accomplished by one stroke of God's magic wand. Some people think Christianity is like Disneyland—the happiest place on earth. They can be extremely disappointed when they realize that believing in Jesus is not a fast pass to the promised land. When I first became a Christian I thought saying "the prayer" was comparable to stepping foot on a boat that cruised smoothly even if a typhoon is on the radar screen. I soon learned that everyone sails rough waters, but who the Captain is makes the difference. Knowing Christ doesn't make life easier, yet it does offer peace in the midst of rough waters. When we come to belief in Christ, life suddenly makes sense, and we find that fulfillment in Christ is the fuel for our lives.

Someone once said, "Runners don't run so they don't have to run anymore; they run so they can run better." I ended up running right back to God. Messing up with Jason didn't destroy me; it simply reminded me in whose arms I belonged.

When I started to write this book, I was overwhelmed with the idea that little-old-me had the responsibility of convincing young people to wait until marriage to have sex. I bit my lip, twirled my hair, and racked my brain for persuasive words, Scripture, and STD statistics. I looked for anything to help me persuade all the vulnerable sex-crazed teens within reach of this book. Yet my attempts seemed too weak to win over my entire generation. I soon realized that what people need is not convincing—but conviction.

Conviction doesn't come from a book; it comes from the Holy Spirit. When I was in a sexual relationship after I became a Christian, I felt badly not because I was breaking the "rules" (in fact, I found a sick sense of satisfaction in breaking rules); I felt badly because I loved God, I knew He loved me, and I wanted to please Him. My purpose was to honor Him, and when I stepped outside that purpose, my life was off balance, and I felt it. I experienced a deep sense of committing adultery against the God I loved. He had plans that I hadn't completely understood; my body was created to worship Him and please Him. Abstinence begins in the heart, and I can't tell my body to refrain from sex unless my heart agrees.

> Flee from sexual immorality. All other sins a man commits are outside his body, but he who sins sexually sins against his own body. Do you not know that your body is a temple of the Holy Spirit, who is in you, whom you have received from God? You are not your own; you were bought at a price. Therefore honor God with your body. (1 Cor. 6:18–20)

When I was at last convicted by God's purposes for me, the spirit inside of me cringed in pain when I dishonored the God who sacrificed His life for mine—the ultimate expression of true love. "Greater love has no one than this, that he lay down his life for his friends" (John 15:13).

If you ask a room full of teenagers what God thinks of sex, many of them will answer, "He thinks it's bad, disgusting, sinful." This is far from the truth. God loves every aspect of sex. He created it and sees it as a beautiful expression of oneness and love. He also knows how the depth of this connection can affect us for good or bad . . . especially when we have sex outside of the way He intended it. Sex is the deepest expression of intimacy here on Earth.

With this in mind—the most powerful emotions, the deepest connection, created by the mightiest God—it is easy to see why God wants sex kept within certain protective boundaries. This boundary is marriage.

> You may say, "I am allowed to do anything." But I reply, "Not everything is good for you." And even

> though, "I am allowed to do anything," I must not
> become a slave to anything. (1 Cor. 6:12 NLT)

God isn't a sadistic rule maker. He didn't tell the earth to circle the sun because He thought it looked cool. He designed an intricate plan for the universe so everything would be aligned. God designed a specific plan for sex, because inside of marriage is the way we'll enjoy it the most. And one of the paradoxical truths about life is that the greatest freedom usually happens within boundaries. Chaos can cause pain, and God's boundaries prevent chaos. If we operate within the border of marriage we'll experience freedom on multiple levels:

Freedom from Shame: If you're married, you can have guilt-free sex. Shame separates us from God and prevents us from receiving His love, forgiveness, and grace. Shame also separates us from each other: you and your partner feel unworthy or "dirty." That's how shame creates a false identity in you. If God is on the "outside" of your relationship, how can you ever be fulfilled if you feel separated from Him?

Freedom from Fear: If you're married there is less fear of pregnancy, disease, or body insecurities. You have the peace of mind that no matter what happens, you have committed to love each other and make it work even through the tough times.

Freedom from Expectations: If you're married you have the rest of your life to develop sexually. There are no insecurities of not feeling good enough. Your partner has committed to be with only you, so you know there will be no comparison between you and the next girl.

I once went out with a guy whom, unfortunately, I'll never forget (partly because his neck and thighs were the size of tree trunks). We were driving along when he turned to me to explain his "dating rule." "Yeah, I don't buy a car unless I test drive it first," he winked (honestly). "Ya know what I mean?"

The "what if I don't like my partner sexually?" idea is absurd for two reasons: (1) chances are that in the beginning of your relationship *neither* one of you will be professionals at making love; and (2) how many partners do you have to test before you find a champion lover? Do *you* want to marry someone who's tested out ninety-nine partners before you, just because he was on a search for personal pleasure? Married couples in a healthy relationship have affirmed to me that their sex life changes and improves as the years go on; in marriage you're allowed to develop, relax, and be yourself.

Freedom from Loss: If you're married, you don't have to worry about breaking up next week after giving away something you can never take back.

I recently took a group of girls to summer camp. Amber was one of my campers. She was the center of attention in more ways than one: her personality was magnetic and her clothes left little to the imagination. Amber was extremely promiscuous, and when I finally got alone with her and mustered up enough courage to question her, I discovered that she didn't really care about sex; she was addicted to the power it gave her. She felt power*less* in her family life, school, and even when she looked in the mirror, and sex gave her authority in her unstable life. She could finally *feel* in control. When she met a guy, she had the influence to seduce, entice, or withhold sex if she pleased. At the end of our conversation I asked her, "How do you feel after you lose your power?" She lowered her head and mumbled, "It happens to me every time." In marriage, you're allowed to be vulnerable and don't have to worry about losing your power.

> But our bodies were not made for sexual immorality. They were made for the Lord, and the Lord cares about our bodies. (1 Cor. 6:13 NLT)

Sometimes we fear that God's hand in our lives will cost us, when in reality it benefits us. God put sexual boundaries in place to protect our bodies and hearts. You probably wouldn't share your deepest secret with someone who isn't a committed friend, so how can it make sense to give your *body* to someone that you may never talk to again? God created sex as a gift for us, but we must be careful to unwrap it as He instructs. These instructions—the "rules" of sex and marriage—are not ones that inhibit us, but rather they empower us to walk in freedom.

You may never find yourself back in your ex-boyfriend's arms, but if you do, you need to remember that it's easy to live for God—on the surface. If we're not consistently going deeper into our relationship with God, we'll soon see the evidence—we all fail without Him. But when we've truly experienced Christ's grace, we can't help but be brought to repentance. It's okay to feel regret over a poor decision; heads hung low is okay for a while. But God has plans, hope, and a future for us, no matter where we are spiritually.

Temptation comes over us like a cozy blanket that feels so good to cuddle with. But when we see it coming, we must cry out quickly to God who says, "No temptation has seized you except what is common to man. And God is faithful; he will not let you be tempted beyond what you can bear. But when you are tempted, he will also provide a way out so that you can stand up under it" (1 Cor. 10:13).

It's true that God will not let us be tempted beyond what we can bear, but we must be responsible to keep ourselves away from situations where we know we're doomed. I should have expected to be tempted when I already had a sexual past with Jason. It's hard—next to impossible, in fact—to say no in the moment, so I recommend that you have a plan before you find yourself in a situation like mine. Prepare yourself by writing on paper your commitment to stay right with God. Ask God in writing to protect you sexually. He delights in protecting His children. Second, tell someone who shares your convictions and beliefs, and ask that person to keep you accountable. Third, in the midst of the pull, cry out to God, and ask Him to give you a way out.

Truth be known, we really *do* want a way out. Knowing we can't find it by ourselves is actually the first step to finding it.

So, Jeremiah, if you're worn out in this footrace with men, what makes you think you can race against horses? (Jer. 12:5 MSG)

In chapter 12, Jeremiah is fed up with watching other people succeed when he's struggling. God then asks him the question in the verse above. In other words, God says, "Stop comparing yourself with people and look to Me for your strength and worth." We are like Jeremiah, trying to become someone or accomplish something in our own strength. We have great ambitions in life (running with horses), but God wants us to understand the basics before we try to save the world. Repentance, grace, and forgiveness are three basics that most Christians struggle with.

The Lord makes decisions about everything from the shape of our toes to the temperature of the sun, yet when He makes a decision to forgive us, we argue with Him. Look at the ocean that covers most of the earth and then just stops at the beach. He commanded in the beginning, "You may come this far and this far only." The Bible says His Spirit hovered over the earth, and then He said, "Let there be light." It's amazing to think about. Yet when He says, "You are a new creation in Christ Jesus, and I have sent your sins as far as the east is from the west," I don't stand in amazement. Instead I cower in shame. Reality is, He says it and it's done. Do you realize that if we refuse to accept grace, we're spitting on Jesus, just like the people did when He was hanging on the cross? We might as well say, "You're crazy. Dying on the cross is a joke, and You don't have the strength to do anything for me. You just aren't powerful enough."

This is life. We fail, and we get back up again. Yet sometimes it's not that easy. Understanding God's grace has always been a struggle for me. We live in a world where nothing is free. It's more comfortable to work for our approval, because then we know we've earned it. The problem with grace is that we *don't* deserve it, we'll *never* earn it, and we *didn't* work for it. Failing our Creator can seem like an unredeemable sin, but we have to set our pride aside and receive His forgiveness with repentance and open arms—and then accept that it's the goodness of God that leads us to repentance (Rom. 2:4).

If we didn't encourage children while they were learning how to walk, if we didn't help them get back up after falling, some would continue to crawl. I recently started believing that I'm not really a "slut on the inside." I'm transformed because of what my Father did for me, and I'm forgiven without a trace of dirt left. He comes and picks up my garbage when I bring it to Him. He took away my stains—past, present, and future. I will continue to fall, and He will continue to help me get back up and to walk with me, teaching me who I am because of Him. We are unconditionally loved by the King of Kings. He not only wants us to learn how to walk after falling down, He wants us to run with Him in confidence.

Will I Ever Love Again?

chapter nine

> The only test as to whether we ought to allow an emotion to have its way is to see what the outcome of the emotion will be. Push it to its logical conclusion and if the outcome is something God would condemn, allow it no more way.
> —Oswald Chambers, *My Utmost for His Highest*[1]

Why is it that most Christian guys I've met are, well . . . not exactly my type? I've had countless conversations with women my age, and this seems to be the common theme: Christian guys act insecure, overemotional, judgmental, and even a little passive.

Not convinced? Below are some entertaining examples from *my* life.

Meet Jon. He has high aspirations of being a pastor and seems emotionally unstable. As tears well up in his eyes, he explains, "God made the grass to be the carpet of the world." Then with great enthusiasm he yells, "Isn't God amazing!? He even thought of grass carpet!" Although I appreciated the zeal, I was thinking, *Puhleeez, God, bring me a normal one!*

Meet Joey. He picks me up for a date, and at the restaurant he's literally twitching, his glance darting everywhere except toward me. Soon he apologizes and asks, "Could you please pray for me right now? I'm really nervous." I stop for a "movie moment"— a moment that seems so unreal, you feel as if you're on-screen. Realizing that I'm still in reality, I swallow the food in my mouth, lucky not to have spit it across the table in disbelief. I ask, "You want me to pray away your nervousness?" Then I actually begin to pray against nervousness in the mighty name of Jesus, all the while thinking, *Buh-bye!*

Meet Abe. We're in ministry together, and after he confesses his feelings for me, I ask him why he thinks we should be together. He responds, "I'm not that picky, and I figure since God put us in each other's paths, I should take advantage of it." Although his deep affections are flattering, I feel about as cherished as his disposable contact lenses. *Not gonna work for me.*

Lastly, meet "Mr. C. C. G." (Creepy Christian Guy) who locks into a probing search of my eyes. With a concerned expression he gently prods, "So what do you struggle with?" As I squirm and try to think of a way to dodge the question, he blurts out, "Well, I struggle with lust!" While this confession might catch laughs in the movie *Anchorman*, it was *not* amusing to me. I realize it's common for a guy to struggle with lust, but it's not okay for him to make this declaration to a girl who doesn't even know his last name.

Where are the good ones? Why isn't it easy and fun to date? Why does it seem that many of us get stuck with either (1) the ones we don't want or (2) the ones we want but aren't good for us spiritually?

"What's the point of sharing these dating disasters?" you ask. The point is, meeting Christians you can't connect with is so disheartening that sometimes men *without* faith look pretty darn good.

In the midst of writing, editing, and submitting this book to publishers I found myself falling for a guy who was really cute, witty, funny, and someone I connected with. He hadn't yet analyzed the grass or asked me to pray away his insecurities. One problem: he didn't know the Lord. His idea of spirituality was listening to Bob Marley while smoking pot. At first I wanted to bang my head against a wall and rip up the pages of this book . . . until I realized this frustration is normal. We're naturally attracted to familiarity, and Bob Marley Guy had a lot of qualities that reminded me of Jason. We're going to be drawn to what we were drawn to in the past.

I have a personal theory that I call "the bad-boy bug": many women want a "bad-boy gone good." If you're like me, you're naturally attracted to certain qualities in the opposite sex: stability, confidence, a connection, intelligence, and, of course, piercing green eyes. If we've broken up with a non-Christian in the past, we're likely to be attracted to one again. There's a sad something inside us that yells, squirms, and whines, "Yes!" when God whispers, "No."

As women, many of us have the dangerous ability to block out reality and see what we want to see. Our minds can miraculously transform any guy into what we think he *could* be. In your journey of moving forward after the breakup, it can be disappointing to continually meet guys who have a list of great qualities but don't know the Lord. As you become frustrated, you may find yourself asking God, "If You are the provider, why aren't You providing?" When loneliness creeps in, it's easy to focus on a guy's charming qualities rather than stressing that your paths are heading in very different directions.

At those times it's tempting to look at a stone and see a loaf of bread. Jesus, as the visible expression of the invisible God, knew better. We have proof that our God is a personal God when we see Jesus going through the same temptations we go through. In our struggle against temptation, it's helpful to see how Jesus responded to temptation. Since He was human, He had longings—just like we do. He struggled against evil in the world, just like we do. In the following story, we see how Jesus responds when He is presented with a substitute for something He needed and longed for.

> Then Jesus was led out into the wilderness by the Holy Spirit to be tempted there by the Devil. For forty days and forty nights he ate nothing and became very hungry. Then the Devil came and said to him, "If you are the Son of God, change these stones into loaves of bread."
> But Jesus told him, "No! The Scriptures say, 'People need more than bread for their life; they must feed on every word of God.'"
>
> (Matt. 4:1–4 NLT)

Jesus was weak from hunger, and I'm sure the Devil's offer sounded pretty good. In desperate situations we may find ourselves tempted, like Jesus, to take control of a situation because we have a longing that screams for satisfaction. Jesus had a physical hunger; we have an emotional hunger to be loved. It seems we'll do almost anything to ease this gnawing ache. Jesus knew He could have easily turned the stone into bread . . . so why didn't He? Jesus trusted His Father. He knew that in perfect time, His Father would provide for His needs. Jesus, just like us, was allowed to lack so that God could provide, and when the provision came, He knew it was from God and not His own strength. With much practice we can eventually become comfortable in living a life entirely dependent on our Father. Jesus knew that He didn't need to transform something it's *not* into something He *wants* when His Father is able to provide the real thing.

But Jesus was also surrounded by people with needs of their own, needs that He recognized and aches that He soothed. We can take comfort in the fact that Jesus not only knows what it's like to suffer need, He is capable of meeting our needs.

That evening the disciples came to him and said, "This is a desolate place, and it is getting late. Send the crowds away so they can go to the villages and buy food for themselves."

But Jesus replied, "That isn't necessary—you feed them."

"Impossible!" they exclaimed. "We have only five loaves of bread and two fish!"

"Bring them here," he said. Then he told the people to sit down on the grass. And he took the five loaves and two fish, looked up toward heaven, and asked God's blessing on the food. Breaking the loaves into pieces, he gave some of the bread and fish to each disciple, and the disciples gave them to the people. They all ate as much as they wanted, and they picked up twelve baskets of leftovers. About five thousand men had eaten from those five loaves, in addition to all the women and children!" (Matt. 14:15–21 NLT)

Jesus doesn't always give us what we want—He gives us what we need. The wonderful thing about God is that He doesn't stop there; He showers us with abundance. Jesus saw the crowd's need. He knew He could have zapped a pile of rocks into bread, but He chose to do something else. He provided bread from bread—the pure ingredients on which our bodies operate most effectively. He took the original, multiplied it, and generously provided.

In the first story Jesus was hungry and incredibly weak after forty days of fasting. He had a legitimate need that could have been met if He had been willing to accept the Devil's offer and settle for a rock. God has access to the best, and you are His child. He says, "He who did not spare his own Son, but gave him up for us all—how will he not also, along with him, graciously give us all things?" (Rom. 8:32).

We're tempted just like Jesus. We're weak and hungry; sometimes the thing to fill our need looks as if it's just within reach.

The guy may not look like what we envisioned but with a little squinting of the eyes we can imagine what he "could be." But if you settle for your imagination, you'll never experience the *reality* of what God has for you. When Jesus provides, He provides the real thing, the raw material, the good stuff, the crème de le crème, the exact thing we need and abundantly.

How, though, do we fight off the urge to make Mr. Wrong feel so like Mr. Right? When I was learning to drive, my dad told me to be a more defensive driver. I learned how to drive on a small island in Washington, where people drive slowly. They wave you in front of them when you turn on your blinker. I never had the need to use my defensive driving skills . . . until I moved to California. I soon realized (ten accidents later) that if I didn't become a defensive driver, I'd be run off the road and left in the dust.

There's a lesson to be learned in defensive driving—about faith and temptation. I had no tools to combat my temptation with the Marley-Lover guy. I couldn't fight my attraction to him on my own.

No soldier goes into battle without his armor, right? Ephesians talks about how this life is a battle and we can't go at it unequipped. We need to learn how to examine the circumstances we find ourselves in and then sharpen our "defensive skills" accordingly.

> And so I insist . . . that there be no going along with the crowd, the empty-headed, mindless crowd. They've refused for so long to deal with God that they've lost touch not only with God but with reality itself. They can't think straight anymore. (Eph. 4:17–19 MSG)

Jesus said if we want to follow Him, we have to pick up our individual crosses. What is your cross? For me, it's wanting love and adoration from a guy, the need for the spotlight, and the impulsive desire to satisfy my screaming flesh. Basically, my cross is *me*. Every day I'm faced with a decision to lay *myself* down and let Him take control. "How?" you ask. As we continue to get to know Him, we will trust Him more. The more we trust Him, the more we'll yield to His way. As we yield to His ways more and more, we come to trust Him even more.

> Be prepared. You're up against far more than you can handle on your own. Take all the help you can get, every weapon God has issued. . . . Truth, righteousness, peace, faith, and salvation are more than words. Learn how to apply them. You'll need them throughout your life. God's Word is an indispensable weapon. (Eph. 6:13–17 MSG)

God has given us a "how to" guide in Ephesians to prepare us for the battles ahead. Each weapon—truth, righteousness, peace, faith, salvation—can be used to fight at the front lines of our weaknesses. When it came to sexual desire and temptation, I felt like I'd been trying to force a plastic lid onto a volcanic eruption. I realized my plan for preventing rebellion was actually enabling it to explode open again and again. I didn't have a plan. We must use God's strategies to get through this life while being protected from harm.

Strategy 1: "Stand your ground, putting on the sturdy belt of truth" (Eph. 6:14 NLT). The Word of God is Truth and that truth can be defined as keeping our hearts and minds in line with God. Concerning my situation with Marley guy, who didn't know the Lord, I got so tied up in my emotions that when I tried to get back to reality, I was caught in a knot of self-deception that I didn't know how to untie. If the truth sets us free, then lies must entrap us. The Bible says, "The heart is deceitful . . . who can know it?" (Jer. 17:9 KJV). Lies and truth get blurred when we believe we *are* what we feel.

Strategy 2: "[Put] on . . . the body armor of God's righteousness" (Eph. 6:14 NLT). Acting on the truth can be the most difficult challenge because usually we know that what we're doing is wrong, yet we choose to do it anyway. This step requires you to take what you know to be true and actually do it.

Strategy 3: *"For shoes, put on the peace that comes from the Good News, so that you will be fully prepared"* (Eph. 6:15 NLT). You may ask, "How does peace protect me?" Peace—or the absence of it—is an indication of whether your decisions are benefiting your spiritual life. Notice that the verse above tells us to "put on" peace. When your thoughts or behavior do not line up with God's will, you'll have lack of peace. Peace, or turmoil, runs parallel to your decisions and is a direct result of your actions. It's a mirror that reflects how your actions are affecting you. If you don't like what you see, it's time to change direction by putting on the "shoes" that allow you to walk in God's direction.

Strategy 4: *"In every battle you will need faith as your shield to stop the fiery arrows aimed at you by Satan"* (Eph. 6:16 NLT). Faith is compared to a shield because it trusts someone stronger and bigger to stand in front of us. This means taking direction from God's Word and trusting that He can see what's ahead. Faith protects us because we are agreeing to follow Someone who will lead us into an ultimately fulfilling life.

Strategy 5: *"Put on salvation as your helmet"* (Eph. 6:17 NLT). Salvation is the ultimate protection because it reminds us of God's great intervention in our lives. We're reminded that we never want to be back where we were before He stepped in. Salvation is a seal that God put on our souls, and it cannot be removed for all of eternity. In the midst of temptation, we can use our salvation as an anchor. Acts 4:12 says, "There is salvation in no one else! There is no other name in all of heaven for people to call on to save them" (NLT). We may know in our minds that there's nowhere better to go than to the Lord, but sometimes it's tempting to run into the wrong arms. In those times, stop and remind yourself of all that God has done to transform you and claim you as His own.

Strategy 6: *"And take the sword of the Spirit, which is the word of God"* (Eph. 6:17 NLT). God's Word has the ability to adjust our wrong thinking into His right thinking. Psalm 119:105 says, "Your word is a lamp for my feet" (NLT). We may not always agree with His advice or plan for our lives, but it's always the best way. The

Bible contains the perfect instructions to teach us how to think, act, live, and love. God's Word protects us and helps us fight back because it filters out the lies and pours in the truth. If we live by His truth, He promises that His plans are "for good and not for disaster, to give you a future and a hope" (Jer. 29:11 NLT).

Strategy 7: "Pray at all times and on every occasion in the power of the Holy Spirit" (Eph. 6:18 NLT). Prayer brings action. John 16:24 reads, "Ask, using my name, and you will receive, and you will have abundant joy" (NLT). Prayer is talking with God, and our conversations with Him fuel our relationship with Him. Prayer protects us because it provides, covers, and heals; it opens our hearts, washes away our shame, keeps us in right thinking, and brings us into His presence.

As Christians, we long for peace, but the truth is we have a real and active enemy. We all know about the armor of God, these weapons against temptation. But just knowing about them isn't enough. If we act passively instead of defensively, we're allowing the enemy to win over our minds, hearts, and souls. Or if we just stand around like protesters holding up our "we want peace" signs, that's the moment the enemy signals for attack. When we stand still, the enemy moves in. We must write the weapons on our hearts and apply them. The list of questions below will help you personally apply each weapon and uncover where you need them in your life.

- How did Jesus stand in a world of weak followers?
- Do my decisions/thoughts bring me closer to the Lord?
- Do my feelings line up with the Word of God?
- Do the outcomes of my actions match up with God's promises for my life?

The armor, the helmet, the shield are all necessary to battle the enemy who tempts us. These defenses protect us from an enemy who attacks at our weakest points. If you reflect on all the "not your types" or the "can't haves" from the past, you'll notice they all have something in common. Every one represents a possible cure for a longing yet to be satisfied. At the root of our pursuit to love again is the desire to be discovered.

I've always assumed that someday someone will discover me. I shudder to write this on paper, but I've felt this way since the glorious original episodes of *90210*. I wrote to "Kelly" from *90210*, sending a desperate letter in which I expressed my desire to *be* someone. I begged her to give me a chance to be discovered, to be famous. I chose "Kelly" simply because she seemed like the best listener out of all the cast members. She had a compassionate character. Soon after I sent my letter, I was dismayed to receive nothing more than a poster with a fake signature scribbled across her chest.

There's a huge part of our souls that longs to be unearthed. The *discoverer* can show up in many different forms. It can come in the form of a lover whom we hope holds the key to unlock the secret room in our souls. Or it can come in the form of a publishing company, TV show, or a stage that has the power to display the fireworks within. The many forms of discoverers came to mind one night when I was about to fall asleep, rotating my ankles in wool socks under a feather comforter: *I'd rather it be a lover instead of a publisher that discovers me.*

It's a lot of effort to be on the prowl. Every time I turn the corner there's a little nagging question: "Could he be the one?" The deeper and more truthful question is, "Could he be the one to fill this empty spot inside of me?" I've always had this fantasy that when we meet we'll lock eyes and we'll just *know* each other. The picture in my head goes something like this: After intense eye contact, we'll somehow find our way to a beach illuminated only by stars. We'll intertwine our fingers and run into an abandoned lifeguard tower. We'll cuddle up with a blanket, conveniently folded over the back of the lifeguard chair. He'll look at me like I am a rare flower species, having the power to cure AIDS. He'll say things that make me want to get up and fly or laugh or something! My eyes become a map to guide his words into the core of my soul, leaving me breathless. We'll talk about things that no one else in the world understands. *Bam*, I'm instantly in *love*!

I imagine that he'll be the only one created on earth who can see the things in me that I'm not capable of seeing in myself. Then reality hits: I roll over to the sound of the coffee maker and look to the vacant pillow next to mine.

Fantasy aside, I confess that when I meet a potential boyfriend, the real me does the following: size up the poor male victim's qualities—the bad, the charming, and the annoying. I make some kind of assessment according to my own messed up idea of what I deserve, need, or desire. Ninety-nine percent of the time I decide he isn't for me. I pick up my emotional backpack, and shove in more loneliness and disappointment. I then strap it back on and walk away with a little less hope in my stride.

When we trust in ourselves alone to judge, we're robbing ourselves. I can't help but believe that today's high divorce rates are partly due to our unrealistic expectations of what a man can fulfill as we enter marriage. My good friend and I have known each other since we were two. For twenty-two years we've been dreaming about marriage. When she got married last summer, her twenty-two years of dreaming culminated in a twenty-five minute ceremony.

I realized that a wedding ceremony is only a twenty-five minute slice of the rest of our lives. A marriage, a man, a TV cast member, a publishing company—anything on this earth for that matter—is capable of failing our expectations. So we must look to God to be the greatest discoverer of our lives.

Instead, we focus on where we're going to meet our discoverer guys. We fantasize about how they'll love us and understand us. But we don't realize that if we aren't fulfilled *before* we meet these discoverers, we won't be *after*. Christ is the ultimate fulfillment, and we often substitute guys. It sometimes takes getting hit over the head to realize that guys can *never* fulfill us if we aren't first fulfilled in Christ.

So, will you ever love again? God created us to be in relationship with one another. God is a good God, and He wants to fulfill our desires as long as they're good for us. Despite our natural longings, it's important to keep God as our God, and not let the search for a relationship become our god.

> For where your treasure is, there your heart will be also. (Matt. 6:21)

> But seek first his kingdom and his righteousness, and all these things will be given to you as well. (Matt 6:33)

If we seek God instead of our physical desire, all of our needs will be met. This is because our longings begin to coincide with God's plan. When we seek God and grow closer to Him, He will shape our desires to align with His, and He will meet them in His way. The more important questions to ask are these: (1) Have I experienced love with my Creator? (2) How do I conform my desires to what God wants for me? (3) How do I live fulfilled in Him alone if my desires aren't met?

The fact that you are single right now could be saving your future marriage. As you grow in your relationship with God, you may look back on your old self and thank God that He allowed you the time to develop who you are without a man by your side. You'll likely go through different phases of singleness; at times you'll love your single life, and other times you'll feel sorry for yourself, crying for a guy to come your way. At one lonely point in this process I decided to trust God with my future guy, and, as cheesy as it may sound, I started a journal for him. When I loathe curling up with my body pillow instead of a warm person, I write to Future Guy and specifically ask God to guide him. If you try it, you'll be amazed at the details that flow out. As idealistic as it may seem, imagine giving that journal to him on your wedding day.

The Lord is the only one who holds the key to unlock the secret rooms within you. Let Him discover you as you discover

Him. If you let a guy define what true love is before God does, you're cheating yourself of Christ's unconditional love. Christ says, "I have called you by name; you are mine" (Isa. 43:1 NLT). He shaped you in His love: "I knew you before I formed you in your mother's womb" (Jer. 1:5 NLT). You are adopted into His family. No one can replace you. No one is like you. Don't let your desire to be discovered lead you to be tempted to settle. Don't let the fantasy take the place of the reality of what God has ready to pour out on you.

You may feel how I did. I'd been doing everything that God asked, walked each step that He led, spent time with Him, relinquished control, and cried out in confusion. I did my best, but it seemed like God was dangling all that I desired just beyond my fingertips. Sometimes it seemed so close I could smell it, and I could imagine what it would feel like to finally hold my long-awaited future in a tight fist. But, once again, I'd be disappointed.

In the face of occasional disappointment He wants to show us that He is a good God. Did you know that when a rose bush grows it's good to cut off the first flowering buds because the middle bloom will be twice the size? God is not satisfied with tiny blooms that spring up quickly. He'd rather be patient and take the time to cut back what's distracting our growth, even if at first it hurts us. He does this so that in the end we can receive the fullness of His plan. Soon, the most beautiful flower unexpectedly surfaces in our life.

"He cuts off every branch of me that doesn't bear grapes. And every branch that is grape-bearing he prunes back so it will bear even more" (John 15:2 MSG). Allow this verse to shape every area of your life. We can live each day in peace when we realize that the pain is not in vain but rather it's all part of a master plan for good from the most loving Father.

We want to be in a relationship with someone who is passionate, and who is determined to live every moment for Christ despite the cost. But in the end, it's not the obtaining of what we want that will amaze us; it's the journey that we took with God to get there. We'll look back and say, "I'm so thankful You pruned the areas where I wanted instant results."

As believers in Christ, we should not be satisfied with tiny curled buds. We know we serve a huge God, who is challenging us to ask Him for what He is capable of giving. What a beautiful life it is when we abandon our ideas of what life in full bloom should look like. What a purposeful life we have when we allow the Gardener to prune what is hard to let go. The roses emerge after the pain.

> My lover said to me, "Rise up, my beloved, my fair one, and come away. For the winter is past, and the rain is over and gone. The flowers are springing up, and the time of singing birds has come, even the cooing of turtledoves. The fig trees are budding, and the grapevines are in blossom. How delicious they smell! Yes, spring is here! Arise, my beloved, my fair one, and come away. (Song 2:10–13 NLT)

Defining the Relationship with God
epilogue

Not long ago, I was in a weird phase. I was curious about, fascinated by, optimistic toward, scared of, and sometimes even horrified of marriage—all at the same time. When I encountered married people, I involuntarily blurted out questions like a hiccup. I was naturally drawn to books and TV shows about the subject. I'd catch myself sitting back, observing dynamics between married couples.

I once heard someone say, "Don't get married unless the two of you can accomplish more together than you can apart." This phrase stuck with me and inspired me to seek a marriage with depth, purpose, passion, and consistent growth together.

I decided a long time ago that I'd rather be single for the rest of my life than be stuck in a relationship where love made up the shallow end of the marriage pool. Who wants to be with a guy who isn't *quite sure* that he wants to be with you? We all want to be with someone who is excited about us and will work hard at cultivating a meaningful relationship.

This desire comes from God, the One who made us in His image. Our desire for deep, meaningful relationships began with Him. He desires such a relationship with us. When He talked to one ancient church that just wouldn't invest itself in a deep mean-ingful relationship with Him, God said, "I know all the things you do, that you are neither hot nor cold. I wish you were one or the other! But since you are like lukewarm water, I will spit you out of my mouth!" (Rev. 3:15–16 NLT).

I recently eavesdropped on a conversation between a wise older woman and a younger woman whose husband was so angry with her that she feared he might divorce her. The older woman knew the couple well, so she consoled her friend: "You won't get a divorce; you love each other dearly. I know he loves you more than anything. He just needs some time to cool down."

Then the young girl cried out in desperation, "But he's the love of my life!"

Her despairing tone made me think of three things: First, this is the kind of love I want—for my husband and I to be so in love that losing each other could potentially destroy our lives. Second, this is rare. I rarely see the flame raging after the commitment is set in stone. I usually see the couple give up on cultivating the relationship because they believe that they're yoked together for-ever and that nothing could possibly go wrong. Third, how did she find this kind of love? Was it luck? Hard work? Faith?

In earlier chapters, I talked about a relationship with God being more fulfilling than a relationship with a guy. If this doesn't make sense to you, then you need to ask yourself about the quality of your relationship with God. Do you know God, or do you just know *of* Him? Do you allow Him to speak to you individually, or do you just learn about Him from your pastor? Do you ask God about important decisions before consulting everyone else? Are you willing to sacrifice and sometimes be uncomfortable in order to do His will?

I know many Christians who have an intoxicating love with Christ, and when I asked them to define such desperate love, two dominant themes emerged: surrender and faith. We must give up on ourselves and surrender to the fact that we are sinners (Isa. 64:6; Rom. 3:23; Titus 3:5), and there's no distance far enough to run away from this reality. But because God loves us, He designed a plan to wash our sin away. He sent His Son to die on the cross, taking it all on Himself. He built a bridge across a canyon of sin that was so wide, no one except Jesus could build it (see chapter 3, "Discovering God's Love").

We must accept what Christ did on the cross and walk across that bridge, entering into a personal relationship with Him. When we "crucify" our own ways and surrender to His, we find ourselves thankful that He doesn't require us to have it all together. When we make the step to give Him control, we realize that we can trust Him (Eph. 2:8–10).

> I have been crucified with Christ and I no longer live, but Christ lives in me. The life I live in the body, I live by faith in the Son of God, who loved me and gave himself up for me. (Gal. 2:20)

When we make a commitment to Christ, we stand before Him and lay our lives in His hands. We become one with Him, and in our hearts we proclaim our vows. But—imagine this scene at the altar:

> Rays of light from the windows illuminate the dust particles. The congregation holds a sea of prayer warriors, family members, warring angels, and everyone she loves. She stands at the altar, where her Creator planned her to be before He uttered the words, "Let there be light" (Gen. 1:3).
>
> The day has come; all of heaven is rejoicing. Tears trickle down her glowing cheeks as she gazes upon the One who unconditionally loved her before she loved Him, the One who relentlessly pursued her up to this very day. She's facing Jesus.

He takes her hand in His, His heart filled with anticipation of the full future before them. Most of all, He is thrilled to love her forever. She finally decides to come face-to-face with the Truth Himself. This day is bigger than she could have ever imagined, and her soul rejoices at spending the rest of her life and eternity with the Lover of her soul.

"I surrender my life to You and I trust You with my heart," she pledges. "Unless I disagree with what You have planned, then I'll have to take things into my own hands."

She continues, "I promise to put no other gods before You . . . unless I fall in love with someone who doesn't encourage these vows I'm making now. Then I'll have to put You on the backburner for a while."

"I'll spend time with You, talking together and studying Your word, so we can get to know each other deeply . . . unless I need to sleep in, or I fill up my schedule with so much busyness that I forget You."

"I vow to love You even when doubts or tragedy fall upon this life . . . unless my best friend dies. Then I'll blame you and turn my back."

This scene sounds absurd, but we're all susceptible to making a conditional commitment. Do our words match our intentions? Do we really mean and understand the commitment we declare to Christ?

In the beginning of our relationship with Jesus we're swept off to the honeymoon. We often assume that it's an easy ride for the rest of the way. Wrong. Eventually the honeymoon ends and, more often than not, so does the commitment. Jesus talks about how His road is narrow and few will find it (Matt. 7:13–14). We get into this "marriage" with Jesus and realize that we're still lazy, selfish, and sinful. We discover that the path can be so narrow that it's easy to lose our footing and fall into the bushes. Any meaningful relationship takes hard work and commitment to last. We are created for a personal relationship with our Creator, and if we're not experiencing the growth and challenges of being filled with His love, there's something coming between us and God.

Not too long ago, I picked up a popular book that includes 276 questions to ask your future husband before you marry him. By about the seventy-second question, my heart started pounding and anxiety took over. It was too much pressure to think about finding someone who answered all the questions to my liking! What if we disagreed on fifty things? One hundred? Does this mean he isn't the one? How do I break it off with someone because we don't agree on what vacations should be like?

Finally I put the book aside and decided to write down my fears about meeting and marrying my potential husband. I knew I needed to face these fears head on and evaluate if they were valid or ridiculous. I feared that my husband and I would just exist together and not grow together. I wondered if my exciting years would be over because of the sacrifices I'd have to make for my partner. I feared that I'd "settle" because I hadn't yet met someone I truly needed or really wanted. I worried that once I made the lifelong commitment, he would take off his game face and put on his mean or uninterested face. I was afraid that I might end up like a slave to my husband instead of a valued, loved, and respected partner recognized for what I bring to the relationship. I feared that I would be expected to look or act a certain way, and if I didn't, he would leave me. I was concerned that I might never be fully understood, or that he wouldn't make any effort to understand me. Most of all, I was terrified of the idea that I might have to give up my dreams.

As I wrote down my fears I realized that some of them were the same fears I felt toward God. I also realized that my panic came, in part, from my having no idea what marriage was supposed to look like in the first place. It can be scary to make a commitment without having the tools to keep it. What's more, it's tough to keep a commitment when we forget why we made it in the first place.

> But I have this complaint against you. You don't love me or each other as you did at first! Look how far you have fallen from your first love! (Rev. 2:4–5 NLT)

I encourage you to remember your "first love" and recall why you committed to Christ in the beginning (if you already have). I invite you to recommit and record that commitment on paper. We can renew our vows to Christ just like married couples often do. Define what this commitment means for your life. Then allow your words to become actions.

Once we've accepted Jesus as our Savior, we become a new person (2 Cor. 5:17) and begin a life of faith in Christ. This faith compels us to act, cultivating our relationship with God on a consistent basis. When we begin to see the result of our faith, our faith grows even more.

One way to cultivate this relationship is by talking and listening. When you're in love with someone you have to communicate! You want to know everything about him. I remember spending hours on the phone with Jason, discussing every detail about our lives. Likewise with God, we must listen to Him; spend time in His Word; maybe join a small group; ask questions; and meditate on, memorize, and apply His words to our lives. We must get to know Him in order to have a strong enough foundation of trust to follow Him. When we receive direction from God, our lives start to make more sense.

We also have to talk to Him. Spend time in prayer, because prayer is the foundation of a deep relationship with God. Be real with Him, and be yourself; He takes us as we are and isn't surprised by anything we have to say. When we share everything with God, we receive comfort.

Another way for a relationship to grow is through giving and receiving. When you're in love you not only want to tell everyone about it, you suddenly want to *do* things for him. Getting involved with a ministry or just sharing your faith allows you to reach a new level of accountability in your faith. Sharing your faith gives you a sense of purpose.

We so easily settle for less, though, than the kind of relationship with God that He offers to us. My great-grandma had a cow named Charlotte. It was my great-grandma's job to take Charlotte out of her pen and lead her to the thick green pasture. Charlotte didn't understand that it took time to get to the pasture, so she'd fight with my great-grandma, pulling against her because she wanted to eat the dying grass right outside her pen. My great-grandma would tell Charlotte, "If you'd only follow me, you'd be better off!" My great-grandma told me that Charlotte just couldn't seem to learn this, but she never gave up trying to lead Charlotte to what was better for her.

Like Charlotte, we see what lies right in front of us and fail to see what lies ahead if we'll only let God lead us there. We miss the wonders of the lush green fields and nibble away on dry, withered grass instead. We miss immersing ourselves in the deep end of the marriage pool with the Lover of our souls.

I'm no longer afraid of marriage. Bringing my fears to God allowed Him to take them away and turn them into a great lesson: I'm already involved in a marriage that requires a great commitment. I challenge you to enter into this marriage with Christ and take it more seriously than anything else in your life. Define the relationship and how deeply you have entered into it with Him. Doing that enables us to be real with Him; we must know where we stand if we desire to move in a direction toward Him.

You are privileged to be the daughter of the most personal King. Learn from the Creator of relationships how to create and keep intimacy. Nourish and protect your commitment to Christ as if it were your last breath. Remember that no guy is worthy of taking the place of Christ, and that a fuzzy feeling from your guy can't compare to the lasting fulfillment Jesus gives. All other loves eventually leave us half empty and thirsting for a drink from the True Source.

Notes

Introduction

1. Robert Robinson, "Come, Thou Fount of Every Blessing," 1758.

Chapter 3: Discovering God's Love

1. Third Day, "Love Song," 1996. All rights reserved. Used by permission.

Chapter 4: Why Should I Break Up?

1. Kahlil Gibran, *The Prophet* (1923; repr. New York: Alfred A. Knopf, 2001), 12.

Chapter 7: Who Am I Without You?

1. John and Stasi Eldredge, *Captivating: Unveiling the Mystery of a Woman's Soul* (Nashville: Nelson Books, 2005), 6–7.

Chapter 9: Will I Ever Love Again?

1. Oswald Chambers, *My Utmost for His Highest* (New York: Dodd, Mead & Co., 1935; London: Oswald Chambers Publication Assoc., 1963), March 22.

95583

Overton Memorial Library
Breaking up :
248.843 W753b 2007

95583